Approved
96th Congress,
2nd Session,
H. Con. Res. 413,
House Doc. No. 96–374

The Capitol

D0117073

Eighth Edition - 97th Congress

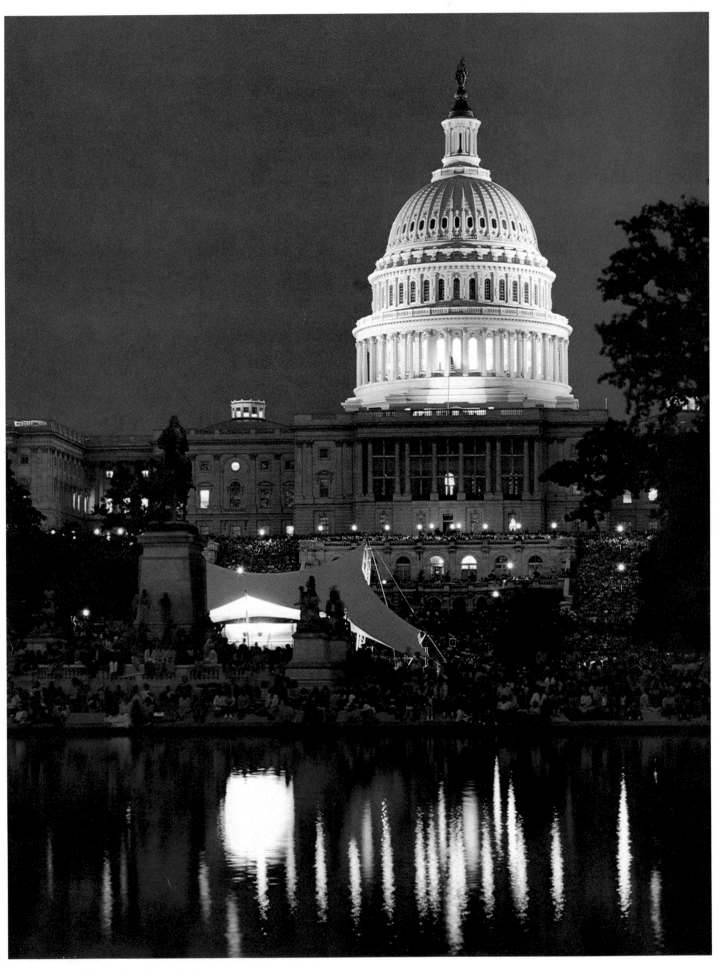

Foreword

This publication, **The Capitol,** is a pictorial history of the Capitol and the Congress of the United States. The late Sam Rayburn, of Texas, Speaker of the House of Representatives, initiated the publication during the Eighty-fourth Congress, and this eighth edition continues to focus not only on the Capitol as a historic ediface but on the Congress as a living and dynamic institution within our Federal Government.

The Capitol of the United States is a renowned landmark, well-known not only to the American people but also to millions of people from other lands. Presidents are inaugurated in front of it; Members of Congress work within it; tourists swarm through it; and artists study it. Within its walls the Legislative Branch of Government—the Congress of the United States—deliberates, debates and decides policies which govern the Nation and, indeed, influence the destiny of the universe.

Construction of the building began in 1793, when President George Washington laid the cornerstone on Jenkins Hill, which was described by Major Pierre Charles L'Enfant, the architect of Washington, D.C., as "a pedestal waiting for a monument." The Capitol was built in five major sections, the first of which was the north wing, which was occupied by Congress and the Supreme Court when the Government moved to Washington from Philadelphia in 1800.

The Capitol not only serves as the seat of our legislature but is also a museum filled with artistic and historic treasures. Included are portraits and statues of past political leaders and of others who have influenced the history of our country. Within the Capitol, primarily in Statuary Hall, which was originally the House Chamber, are statues from every State in the Union. These are inspiring reminders of our forefathers and their contribution to the growth of this great Nation.

This eighth edition of **The Capitol** has been compiled under the joint direction of the Senate Committee on Rules and Administration and the House Committee on House Administration. But the successful compilation of any publication includes the efforts and talents of many individuals. In that context, Chairmen Charles McC. Mathias, Jr., of Maryland, and Augustus F. Hawkins, of California, and the Members of both of the aforementioned committees wish to recognize and express their appreciation for the dedication and cooperative teamwork of the committees' staffs.

Appreciation also goes to those in the Office of the Architect of the Capitol, the Congressional Information and the Typography and Design Divisions of the Government Printing Office, the Congressional Research Service of the Library of Congress, the White House Photographic Service Department, the Senate and House Photographic Studios, and the United States Capitol Historical Society, all of whose assistance was notably helpful.

Senate Committee on
Rules and Administration

House Committee on
House Administration

Chairman
Senator
Charles McC. Mathias, Jr.
(R) Maryland

Senator
Wendell H. Ford
(D) Kentucky

Chairman
Representative
Augustus F. Hawkins
(D) California

Representative
Bill Frenzel
(R) Minnesota

The Capitol—Its History and Architecture

Symbol of The Power of The People

The Capitol of the United States represents Government of the people, by the people, and for the people.

Inception and Growth

The announcement for the Capitol Competition of 1792 offered a lot in the city and $500 for the winning design.

The U.S. Capitol is the embodiment of the ideals and history of this country; the massive cast iron dome has become a symbol that has worldwide recognition. Millions visit the Capitol each year, and their memories are imprinted with the bustle of the House of Representatives and Senate, the incomparable view down the Mall from the West Front terraces, and the magnificence of the Rotunda, Statuary Hall and works of art. To those whose acquaintance with the Capitol is drawn from photographs in books, newspapers, and magazines, or from television and radio broadcasts, the great State occasions that take place in the building may seem most compelling. These Americans are more likely to remember ceremonies such as inaugurations, the Presidents' annual state of the Union messages, or the moments of national grief when our greatest citizens have lain in state in the Rotunda. The Capitol is an extraordinary repository of art and craftsmanship, the seat of Congress, and a living structure; it is one which has been designed, built, rebuilt and inhabited over the years by lively, colorful, and dedicated people.

At the time of its inception, the Capitol seemed to many people to be an overly ambitious project for the United States to undertake. In 1792 the Commissioners of the District of Columbia announced a competition to select a design for the building which would house Congress, the Library of Congress and the Supreme Court. A very satisfactory plan for the President's House by James Hoban, an Irish-born architect who had settled in America, had already been accepted. While the competition for the Capitol Building produced some interesting designs, it presented nothing that seemed appropriate to the building's complex function and symbolic purpose. America's few architects were mostly self-trained men whose experience was limited primarily to homes or small-scale public buildings, and neither President Washington nor Secretary of State Thomas Jefferson was satisfied with the various designs submitted by the July 15th deadline.

In November of the same year, William Thornton, a young multi-talented physician, wrote to the Commissioners of the Federal District, asking permission to submit a late entry. Thornton was an accomplished artist and amateur architect, and had also taken part in the earliest steamboat experiments in America. Since leaving Philadelphia

Thomas Jefferson oversaw both competitions for the construction of the Capitol and the White House. This sketch was probably done about 1799 by Benjamin Latrobe, the Second Architect of the Capitol.

Although Thomas Jefferson did not enter the competition for the Capitol he did draw this theoretical plan. A student of antiquity, he used the perfect form, the circle, as the basis for his study.

in 1790, he had been living in his native Virgin Islands. Thornton's request was granted, and he returned at once to Philadelphia, submitting his design to President Washington in January 1793. Washington was immediately impressed with the design, and soon wrote praising the plan for its "grandeur, simplicity, and beauty of the exterior". Thomas Jefferson eagerly concurred, writing that "Dr. Thornton's plan has . . . so captivated the eyes and judgment of all as to leave no doubt you will prefer it when it shall be exhibited to you". The finished version of his design delighted everyone except the runner-up, Stephen Hallet, a French-born architect who had seemed assured of winning the competition before Thornton's entry was submitted. As compensation, Hallet was awarded a $500 prize, the same as that granted Dr. Thornton, and he was placed in charge of actual construction of the Capitol,

thus initiating one of the many personality conflicts that attended the planning and design of the new Capitol.

As early as 1783, the Continental Congress had resolved to establish two capital cities, one of which was to be located on the Potomac near Georgetown. The idea of a second city, which would have been located on the Delaware River above Trenton, New Jersey, had been discarded, and by January 1791 Major Pierre L'Enfant was appointed to design the new Federal City. Three months later George Washington issued a proclamation establishing the District of Columbia location.

Unfortunately, L'Enfant's temperament frequently placed him in conflict with his associates. One of these was Squire Daniel Carroll, an original landowner in the District of Columbia, who decided to build a new manor house on the site of one of the

Stephen Hallet was the runner-up for the Capitol Competition (1792). This elevation shows the basic idea for the building's eventual construction. Thornton saw Hallet's work before making his own winning design.

This design for the East Front was drawn by Dr. Thornton and approved by George Washington. The wing on the right was completed first.

On September 18, 1793, President George Washington laid the Capitol's cornerstone. This event was captured by artist Allyn Cox in the first floor corridor of the House Wing (1974).

great avenues that L'Enfant planned to radiate in all directions from the Capitol. Unwilling to accept this intrusion on his grand design, L'Enfant sent a work crew to demolish the unfinished mansion which stood in the way of what would eventually become New Jersey Avenue. But Squire Carroll's uncle was also one of the three commissioners charged with the development of the city; combined with L'Enfant's other continuing disputes with the commissioners, this affair led to his dismissal by President Washington.

President Washington formally approved Dr. Thornton's revised design for the Capitol Building, and on September 18, 1793, he laid the Capitol's cornerstone in a Masonic ceremony in company with local officials. After the ceremony, in which the cornerstone was placed on a silver plate, an ox was roasted on a spit, and the assembled multitude ate and drank heartily until dusk. That event was both the first and last recorded occasion on which the cornerstone with its engraved silver plate was seen. In 1958, during the extension of the East Front, a determined but unsuccessful effort was made to find the stone.

Construction of the Capitol proceeded steadily after the festivities of the cornerstone-laying were over. Throughout this period a conflict was brewing between Dr. Thornton, who sought to preserve his design intact, and Stephen Hallet, the supervisor of construction, who began to introduce subtle changes in the design which were reminiscent of his own rejected plan. Thornton forced a confrontation, and the outraged Hallet was dismissed in 1794. The next superintendent of construction was George Hadfield, who arrived in 1795. Almost immediately he came under Dr. Thornton's criticism; Hadfield, though talented and dedicated, overstepped his authority, and he was dismissed three years later. In 1800, Congress was installed in the one completed wing of the Capitol.

In 1803 President Jefferson appointed Benjamin Latrobe, an academically trained architect, to oversee the continuing construction of the Capitol. Since December 1802, the House had been meeting in a temporary brick structure thrown up hastily on the foundations of its own wing. One story tall, oval and unbearably hot three seasons of the year, this structure was called "the Oven" by the Representatives who were unfortunate enough to meet in it. One of Latrobe's first acts was to order the demolition of "the Oven", and to raise the walls of the House wing. Work on it proceeded smoothly under Latrobe's guidance, but his prolific production of designs for other public and private buildings frequently directed his attention away from Washington, engendering considerable criticism. In response, he appointed a fellow Englishman, John Lenthal, to be Clerk of the Works, with day-to-day responsibility for the Capitol when he himself was away. Lenthal took charge of the work with vigor, competence, and ability, but during one of Latrobe's extended absences in 1808, he removed the supports for the vaulting in the Supreme Court Chamber prematurely. The massive arches collapsed, killing Lenthal.

Upon the completion of the House wing, Latrobe substantially rebuilt the Senate wing which was plagued with leaks and falling plaster, although less than ten years old. His revised plan featured a handsome two-story Senate Chamber directly over the ground floor chamber of the Supreme Court. Both halls were recently restored as

This is the Capitol when first occupied by Congress in 1800. The Supreme Court Chamber was on the first floor and the Senate Chamber occupied the second floor. Both Chambers have been restored.

part of the Capitol's Bicentennial program, and are now open to visitors.

Under Latrobe's continued supervision, the House and Senate wings of the Capitol were virtually finished by 1811. Yet due to the imminence of war with Great Britain, the general appropriations for work on the Capitol ceased, and all plans for further improvement were put aside. In August of 1814, a British fleet appeared in the Chesapeake Bay with the determined purpose of capturing Washington; they brushed aside the opposing American militiamen at Bladensburg, and on the 24th of that month, marched into the Federal City. One of the British commanders, Rear Admiral Cockburn, led his men into the House Chamber, jumped up onto the Speaker's chair, and called the troops around him. Mocking legislative procedure, he asked the soldiers: "Shall this harbor of Yankee democracy be burned? All for it say 'aye'." The Admiral's motion passed unanimously, and the British troops set a great bonfire by piling desks, carpets, books, paintings, and everything else movable in the center of the Chamber, insuring a good blaze by sprinkling gunpowder over the pile before setting the torch to both wings. Late in the evening a violent thunderstorm drenched the burning buildings, saving them from total destruction.

Latrobe made several drawings that showed the extent of the damage, and then proceeded with reconstruction of the Capitol and the President's House; the exterior walls of both buildings were painted to hide the stains and scars left by the fires. Latrobe used that opportunity to alter Thornton's plan to his own tastes. He set to work with characteristic vigor, designing an enlarged Senate Chamber and a handsome semicircular room for the House of Representatives, which today is Statuary Hall. During the reconstruction, Congress met in a building where the Supreme Court now stands. This structure, the "Brick Capitol", was hastily erected in 1815 at the expense of some of Washington's businessmen, who feared that Congress would move the seat of Government away from the District of Columbia.

After Latrobe's resignation in 1817, Charles Bulfinch of Boston became

"Burning of the Capitol" depicted in mural by Allyn Cox, in the House corridor (1974).

This original drawing of the Capitol depicts the damage it sustained after it was burned by the British during the War of 1812.

Benjamin Latrobe proposed a Propylea type entrance for the West Front. Subsequently this part of the Capitol was altered and extended by Bulfinch.

9

For nearly 50 years this is where the Representatives met. This painting by Samuel F. B. Morse shows a night session of the House in 1822. The thick hangings deadened unwanted echoes.

This is the earliest known photograph of the Capitol. It is a daguerreotype and was probably taken by John Plumbe, Jr., reproduced in a lithographic print (called a Plumbeotype) and published around 1846. Water for non-culinary purposes was stored in the cistern seen in the center foreground.

the third architect to shape the Capitol. Widely respected for his designs, which included the State Houses for Massachusetts and Connecticut and a number of hospitals, Bulfinch also appears to have possessed the tact and political sensitivity his predecessors had lacked. He served as Architect from 1818 until the Capitol was completed in 1829, when the position of Architect of the Capitol was abolished. It was Bulfinch who completed the central section of the building, including the lower walls of the handsome Rotunda familiar to tourists today. Although most of his work was done according to plans prepared by Latrobe, Bulfinch was able to put his personal stamp on the building in his execution of the extended West Front and the dome. Much criticism had been directed at the low height of the Rotunda dome as originally planned, and Bulfinch prepared several drawings of alternate solutions to the problem, including one dome of considerably greater height merely as a point of comparison. Upon submission of these designs to the Cabinet, the taller dome was selected as the most attractive solution despite Bulfinch's personal distaste for the design. He was ordered to go ahead with construction of the higher dome, built of masonry and wood with copper sheathing.

During the reconstruction after the fire, Congress decided to assign watchmen to keep strangers from wandering throughout the Capitol and grounds at night. Three watchmen and

one sergeant were hired in 1825; they constituted the first police force in the Federal District outside Georgetown, and were the forerunners of today's U.S. Capitol Police. These early watchmen served also as guides in the Capitol. With the influx of visitors from the Centennial Exposition in Philadelphia in 1876, a separate guide force was recruited, thus beginning the present day guide service.

In 1824 the Marquis de Lafayette, hero of the Revolution, returned to America for his first visit in forty years. The great general was given a warm welcome everywhere he traveled in the country, but nowhere was it more spontaneous or heartfelt than in the Chamber of the House of Representatives, where he was received by the Members on December 9, 1824. Unprompted, they rose to their feet to honor him, and then, as though two hundred men were a single person, they doffed their hats. This was a remarkable tribute according to the customs of the day. Members of Congress usually removed their hats only in the presence of the President, a reigning monarch, clergyman, or, of course, when meeting a lady. The rules of the House no longer allow hats to be worn in the chamber.

Benjamin Latrobe's design for the reconstructed Capitol had included an important innovation, the Capitol's first sanitary facilities. Originally the Congress was accommodated for nearly two decades with facilities outside the building; in the delicate lan-

10

guage of the time, they were known as "neccessaries". Latrobe, with characteristic ingenuity, provided water closets in the courtyards and in the Capitol. Water was carried to the roof of the building from nearby cisterns and poured down the drains, which emptied at the foot of Capitol Hill. Before Washington had a city water system a large circular cistern on the East Front was kept filled with water for non-culinary use.

Washington was a small town, with little in the way of entertainment other than the business of legislation and government. Consequently, viewing the Congress while in session was one of the most important and liveliest diversions of the day. Ladies of the city frequently spent their afternoons in the House and Senate visitors' galleries watching the parliamentary maneuvering and debates. The Senate, in particular, was considered worthy of attendance; Henry Clay, John C. Calhoun, and Daniel Webster, three of the greatest orators in our history, were all Members of the Senate in the decades before 1850. On the day a burning issue was to be debated, the galleries in the Senate would begin to fill early in the morning; when the time came for the debate to begin, the more gallant Members of the Senate would give up their desks to the belles who could not crowd their way into the galleries. On warm days, the poorly ventilated Chamber would heat up quickly, and fruit and beverages were sometimes passed on long poles to the sweltering spectators.

Sam Houston, the father of Texas' independence and statehood, was a colorful Senator of this era. He would lounge at his desk with the casual air of a frontiersman, whittling delicate wooden hearts which he passed up to the loveliest ladies in the gallery. He disdained the black broadcloth tail coats favored by many of his colleagues in favor of a more flamboyant wardrobe. A visitor once noted that his costume included a panther-skin vest, a brightly striped serape slung over his shoulder, and a generous sombrero.

The crypt with its 40 Doric columns supports the Rotunda which is directly above it. Built by Bulfinch, it is a showcase for its natural sandstone construction.

An oil painting by an unknown artist depicts the Capitol from Pennsylvania Avenue about 1827.

An 1842 session in the Senate is illustrated in this old print. On the basis of this and others, information was ascertained that enabled restoration of the Chamber in 1976.

11

The House of Representatives had its own characters in those lively years. One of the best-remembered was John Randolph of Virginia, a member of the famous family that provided both the Old Dominion and the United States with a number of outstanding public servants. John Randolph served in the House and Senate almost continuously from 1799 until his death in 1833, but his first love was always hunting. At the height of the hunting season, it was his regular practice to ride to the hounds from dawn until the hour the House's session began. At the appointed time, he would gallop to the Capitol; "leaving his lathered horse with grooms, Randolph would then stride into the House Chamber, still clothed in mud-spattered boots and red hunting coat, with a pack of hounds padding along at his heels".

During those years the atmosphere within the grand space of the Rotunda was also far different from its present august dignity. Numerous vendors hawked items ranging from food to souvenirs. Petitioners and office-seekers trailed Congressmen as they moved in and out of the legislative chambers and committee rooms. Temporary exhibits displaying the latest innovations in science, agriculture, or industry attracted various passers-by. In both House and Senate restaurants, refreshments were liberally and regularly enjoyed by thirsty legislators, despite the fact that the American Congressional Temperance Society had

been established in the House Chamber itself in 1833. A few years later, the Senate voted to ban the sale of hard liquor in the Capitol. The House refused to go along, and for seven years, the Senate abided by its own resolution while the other side of the building continued to flow with strong drink.

The most pervasive habit of the time, if we are to accept accounts of contemporary European travelers in America, was the use of tobacco in the form of chewing or snuff. Both men and women seem to have enjoyed those forms of tobacco. Charles Dickens wrote: "Washington may be called the headquarters of tobacco tinctured saliva . . . In all public places of America, this filthy custom is recognized."

One thing foreign visitors did agree upon was the grandeur of the Capitol itself. Mrs. Frances Trollope, an English visitor noted for her acid pen, appeared to be happily surprised by the building:

"Our first object the next morning was to get sight of the Capitol, and our impatience sent us forth before breakfast. The mists of morning still hung around this magnificent building when first it broke upon our view, and I am not sure that the effect produced was not the greater for this circumstance. At all events, we were struck with admiration and surprise. None of us, I believe, expected to see so imposing a structure on that side of the Atlantic. I am ill at describing buildings, but the beauty and majesty of the American capitol might defy an abler pen than mine to do it justice. It stands so finely, too, high and alone.

"The magnificent western facade is approached from the city by terraces and steps of bolder proportions than I ever before saw. The elegant eastern front, to which many persons give the preference, is on a level with a newly-planted, but exceedingly handsome enclosure, which in a few years, will offer the shade of all the most splendid trees which flourish in the Union. . . ."

The Capitol was the scene of many "firsts" in American history. In 1829, in a ceremony open to the public, Andrew Jackson became the first President to be inaugurated on the East Front steps. Until that time, chief executives had been installed either in the Senate or House of Representatives' Chamber, with only invited guests being admitted. Old Hickory

Clio, the Muse of History, in her chariot, notes significant events as they transpire. The clock was once the official timepiece of the House.

In 1829 Andrew Jackson was inaugurated as the seventh President of the United States on the East Front steps of the Capitol. This event was captured in a painting by artist Allyn Cox in the first floor corridor of the House Wing (1974).

would have none of that; he had been elected as a man of the people and he was determined to have his installation open to everyone. Six years later, President Jackson was the first victim of an assassination attempt at the Capitol. On January 30, 1835, Jackson attended funeral services in the Capitol. As he was leaving the Rotunda to return to the White House, a man accosted him, raised a pistol, and fired point blank at the President. The weapon misfired; Jackson, no stranger to a good scuffle, went after the would-be assassin with his cane. A second pistol also misfired, and the President and a navy lieutenant succeeded in disarming the assailant.

John Quincy Adams has the distinction of being one of two Presidents who was elected to Congress after leaving the White House. The other, Andrew Johnson, was elected to the Senate but served only a short time before his death. Adams continued to serve with great distinction for seventeen years; he was stricken on the floor of the House in 1848 while delivering an impassioned attack on the treaty which had just ended the Mexican War. The old patriot was carried from the floor to the Speaker's office where he died two days later. A bronze disc was set into the floor of the old House chamber to mark the site of his desk. It remains today, not only as a tribute to Adams, but also to mark the famous "whispering spot", where words spoken softly can be heard all the way across the room.

The Capitol is seldom thought of as a scientific laboratory, but it was there in 1844 that Samuel F. B. Morse first demonstrated the telegraph. Forty miles of wire had been strung to Baltimore, where his assistant waited with a receiving set. Morse tapped out the historic message: "What hath God wrought?" From Baltimore Morse's assistant stoically flashed in return, "What is the news in Washington?"

By the eighteen-forties, it was apparent that Congress was outgrowing the Capitol. When Dr. Thornton had submitted his design in 1792, the Senate consisted of 30 Members, and the House 106. The results of the 1850 census caused the House to be enlarged to 237 Members, and the 31 States of the Union sent 62 Senators to Washington. Thus Congress had more than doubled, and the country had spread across the continent. It was obvious that the Capitol would have to be enlarged; Senator Jefferson Davis of Mississippi, who became President of the Confederacy, served as a persuasive spokesman for those Members of both Houses favoring expansion. In September 1850, Congress appropriated funds for design and construction of two large new wings. The architect chosen for the new wings was Thomas U. Walter of Philadelphia, who was already supervising construction of the

In 1835, after attending the funeral for a Member of Congress, President Andrew Jackson was rushed on the steps of the Capitol by a would-be assassin. The President escaped death because both guns of the attacker misfired.

The Old Supreme Court Chamber.

Robert Mills, architect of the Treasury Building and the Washington Monument, was an unsuccessful competitor for the 1850 Extension project. This view from the Senate end of the Capitol shows his idea for a dome.

Treasury Building near the White House. Massachusetts and Maryland marble were selected for construction of the new wings in place of the Virginia sandstone used in the old Capitol. The official cornerstone-laying for the new wings occurred on July 4, 1851, when President Millard Fillmore presided over the ceremony wearing the same Masonic apron that President Washington had used six decades earlier. But the real highlight of the day was the principal address delivered by old "Black Dan" himself, Daniel Webster. Webster, then Secretary of State, had spent most of the previous thirty years in the House and Senate. Against the background of worsening relations between the North and South, Webster's speech became a plea for the preservation of the Union. Of the three former rhetorical "giants" of the Senate, Calhoun was dead, Clay was near the end of his brilliant career, and Webster himself was in the final year of his life.

If the future of the Republic seemed in doubt, that of the Capitol was not. Thomas Walter pressed ahead with the new Senate and House wings; by late 1857, the House of Representatives moved into its new Chamber, and in January of 1859, the Senate occupied the north wing, although much embellishment and decorative work remained to be done. It had been apparent almost from the beginning of the expansion that despite the intentional visual harmony of the new and old sections, the Bulfinch dome was dwarfed by the bulk of the enlarged Capitol. The decision was made to replace the dome with one more proportionate to the whole structure, one which was in fact nearly twice as high as the old Bulfinch dome. Walter drew on elements present in several of the great domes of the Old World—for example, St. Peter's in Rome and St. Paul's in London—to produce the masterpiece that today is instantly recognizable world-wide.

In an early model the allegorical female figure representing "Freedom" wore a liberty cap inspired by antique classical models and associated with freedom from slavery. Secretary of War Jefferson Davis objected to that symbolism from the Southern point of view that such a depiction would only further inflame the pro- and anti-slavery passions that were sweeping the country in the mid-nineteenth century, and so Thomas Crawford, the sculptor, altered his design, substitut-

Thomas U. Walter, the fourth Architect of the Capitol, was originally hired as the Architect of the Extension. This 1851 elevation shows the proposed new House and Senate Wings. The Bulfinch dome is still visible in this drawing.

Daniel Webster delivered a two hour oration at the Corner Stone Laying Ceremony for the Extension in 1851.

Influence of classic architecture on U.S. Capitol. (L. to R.) St. Paul's Cathedral, London; U.S. Capitol; St. Peter's Cathedral, Rome; all drawn to same scale. The grandeur of the two cathedral domes undoubtedly influenced Thomas U. Walter's design for the dome of our Capitol.

ST. PAUL'S   U.S. CAPITOL   ST. PETER'S

ing a helmet surmounted by an eagle's head and feathers, and encircled with stars.

Crawford's statue of "Freedom" was fortunate to arrive in America at all. The sculptor modeled the statue in his studio in Rome; in April 1858, his full-size plaster model was shipped from Leghorn, Italy, for casting in America. The boat carrying the statue was so old and slow that it took a full month to cross the Mediterranean, and even then was forced to put in at Gibraltar for the repair of her many leaks. After a month in Gibraltar, the ship sailed again for New York, and this time made it as far as Bermuda, where the leaks were judged so extensive that the ship was pronounced a total loss and sold. It was not until December 1858, that "Freedom" arrived in New York, and it was to be another five years before she was cast in bronze and placed on the tholos of the Capitol dome.

The enlarged Capitol offered legislators a luxury of space on a scale that was not possible in the old building. Ample offices were provided for principal officers of both Houses, while comfortable lobbies were included for the relaxation of Senators and Representatives. Another innovation in 1859 was the installation of marble bathtubs. In the days when many Senators and Representatives lived in rooming houses and hotels that boasted few amenities, the handsome marble tubs, located in the Capitol basement, pro-

This is a rare photograph of a detail of Thomas Crawford's "Freedom". Commissioned in 1856, the statue was raised into place on top of the dome in 1863.

Drawn by Thomas U. Walter this study shows the skeletal arrangement of the dome's interior ironwork.

Architect Thomas Walter's sketch in 1860 compares elevation and profiles of the dome.

This cross-section rendering of the dome was prepared in 1859.

After extensive study the dome was constructed as shown in this drawing.

The Hall of Columns is located on the first floor of the House Wing. The marble and bronze statues are part of the National Statuary Hall Collection.

The assault on Senator Sumner by a Member of the House of Representatives is depicted in this 1856 edition of "Frank Leslie's Illustrated Newspaper".

vided a popular service. Two are left, but they are in unusable condition in a basement office used by Senate engineers.

During the eighteen-fifties, the argument over slavery grew in intensity, and Daniel Webster's worst fears were borne out. Congress had always been "rough-and-tumble"; Vice President Martin Van Buren had occasionally worn a brace of pistols thrust in his belt while presiding over the Senate. Tempers flared frequently, and a Senator from South Carolina wrote that "every man on the floor of both Houses is armed with a revolver". On May 20, 1856, Senator Charles Sumner of Massachusetts rose to denounce Senator A. P. Butler's stand on the Kansas-Nebraska Act, which had repealed the Missouri Compromise and instead made it theoretically possible for the Nebraska Territory to enter the Union as a slave State. He characterized Senator Butler, an aging South Carolinian, as a Don Quixote who made vows to a mistress, "though polluted in the sight of the world, is chaste in his sight. I mean the harlot, slavery". Two days later, in the nearly empty chamber, Sumner was approached at his desk by Representative Preston Brooks of South Carolina, a kinsman of Senator Butler. Brooks said, "I have read your speech twice over carefully; it is a libel on South Carolina, and Mr. Butler, who is a relative of mine." Without another word, Brooks began to beat Senator Sumner with his heavy, metal-capped walking stick. Brooks continued to strike the Massachusetts Senator until he fell unconscious. Sumner's injuries were so severe that it was several years before he could return to his duties.

The inevitable rupture came in 1861, when Senators and Representatives from States which had seceded resigned from Congress and left Washington. When the first influx of volunteers from the northeastern States began to pour into Washington, troops were billeted in the Capitol, since Congress was not in session at the time. A bakery was established in the basement to feed the Union troops their daily ten-ounce bread ration. President Lincoln had originally asked for 75,000 volunteers willing to serve for ninety days, but it soon became apparent that the war would be a long and hard-fought struggle. The carefree young men who had camped out in the Rotunda were molded into hardened soldiers by the time the Second Battle of Manassas and the Battle of Antietam were fought in 1862. Thousands of wounded men from the two engagements spilled into Washington, filling the Army hospitals which had been established in public buildings. In the midst of the emergency, the Capitol was again employed: fifteen hundred cots were set up in its great open spaces, and they were quickly filled with wounded soldiers.

Numerous anecdotes are preserved which reflect the intense emotions of this period. Early in the conflict, a Union Army private mounting guard at the Capitol was shown the Senate Chamber desk occupied by Senator Jefferson Davis in the years before the war. In an outburst of frustrated rage, he thrust his bayonet deeply into the dark mahogany desk. The damage has long since been skillfully repaired.

Throughout these trying months, work on the great cast iron dome had gone ahead under Thomas Walter's direction. Colonel Montgomery Meigs, Chief of the Army Corps of Engineers, had halted construction for a short

time during the summer of 1861, but President Lincoln's personal determination to see the Capitol completed had prevailed. He was once asked by a visitor, John Eaton of Ohio, how he could justify the continued construction of the building, especially of the cast iron dome. Lincoln calmly replied that the work must continue. "If the people see the Capitol going on, it is a sign that we intend the Union shall go on." In late 1863, the President must have felt supremely vindicated: that year brought victories at Vicksburg and Gettysburg which pointed the way to ultimate triumph for the Union. On December 2nd, while he himself lay in bed with a fever, a huge crowd gathered in the Capitol Plaza to watch while the sections of Thomas Crawford's statue of "Freedom" were raised to the summit of the dome and bolted together. Upon the completion of the task, a tremendous salute was sounded from the guns of the 12 surrounding forts that protected Washington.

During the Civil War the Rotunda became a field hospital. Work on the dome was halted for a while but the elaborate scaffolding needed for its construction was left in place. Allyn Cox recorded this moment as part of the decorations for the House corridor (1974).

This 1863 drawing by Architect Walter shows the head of Thomas Crawford's "Freedom" being raised into place atop the new cast iron dome.

During the Civil War parts of the Capitol were used for the troops. In this view supplies are shown stored under the Senate Chamber while bread ovens were in rooms on the basement floor.

The Capitol in Various Stages of Growth

Early photograph of the Capitol about 1850. Note the small wrought iron balcony on the Senate side. A connecting corridor and the present Senate wing now obliterate this view of the original north wing.

New Senate wing nearly completed, the House wing and the dome still under construction. In May 1861 the "Illustrated London News" carried this woodcut. It was slightly in advance of the actual progress as the Senate steps and portico had not progressed this far. Tiber Creek runs down the mall toward the half completed Washington Monument.

The Capitol, 1861. Less than a month after Lincoln was inaugurated the first time, the Civil War broke out and troops were called to protect the Capitol. Statuary for the Senate pediment and troops drilling on the east lawn were all part of the Capitol scene this May day of 1861.

House wing under construction. With the extension of the building it was necessary to remove the iron Bulfinch gates and enlarge the grounds. Three of the supporting square posts are now located on Constitution Avenue.

By water to the Capitol in 1860. From the White House side or mall end this was the scene more than 100 years ago, showing the old canal and the Botanic Garden.

A marble monolithic column for the Senate portico is swung into place. In the background the dome nears completion.

"Hope Protecting Genius", the first figure of the House pediment, is ready to be hoisted into position. The completed grouping is known as "The Apotheosis of Democracy", and the original models may be seen in the Capitol terminal of the Rayburn subway.

Horsecars at the Capitol (Summer 1862). The horsecar line ran across the east plaza. Blocks of marble are visible in the foreground but construction is completed.

Pediment of the House wing nears completion. The sculptural work by Paul W. Bartlett was authorized in 1908 and the unveiling ceremony took place in 1916. Here craftsmen are about to put another allegorical figure into position.

Capitol Interiors

The elaborate corridor paintings in the Senate Wing are the work of Constantino Brumidi.

Before Brumidi began painting the frieze in the Capitol, he rendered a 24 foot preliminary drawing. The section of it shown depicts "Pizarro's Conquest of Peru, 1533".

In 1864 the Congress came up with the answer to one of the most annoying problems raised by the enlargement of the Capitol, the question of what was to be done with the Old House Chamber. The Senate had previously reassigned its former quarters to the Supreme Court, which occupied the former Senate Chamber until 1935. The House Chamber was another matter: it was too large to be used for any subsidiary function, too handsome a room to subdivide into office space, and traffic between the House and Senate Wings passed directly through it. After 1857, the House almost seemed to forget its existence, and the Chamber fell into disuse and disrepair. Old furniture, boxes, bales and other unwanted material were stored in its corners. In 1864, Representative Justin Morrill, author of the Morrill Act which provided for land grant colleges, rose in the House to offer a solution to the dilemma: "To what end more useful or grand, and at the same time simple and inexpensive, can we devote it [the old Chamber] than to ordain that it shall be set apart for the reception of such statuary as each State shall elect to be deserving of this lasting commemoration?" His proposal became law on July 2, 1864, and thus the Statuary Hall was born. A statue of Rhode Island's fighting Quaker general of the Revolution, Nathanael Greene, was the first to be placed in the Hall.

In time, there came to be almost a forest of statues of every size in the Hall, and in the early 1930s, engineers discovered that their enormous weight was endangering the structure of the floor, the Hall being in one of the oldest parts of the building. In 1933, provision was made for relocation of as many statues as necessary to relieve pressure on the foundation. Statuary Hall did not change substantially again until the 1970s, when Congress decided to restore, insofar as possible, the room to its original appearance as the House Chamber. A number of statues were relocated, and the remainder rearranged in a more attractive pattern. The handsome half-dome that had replaced the original was decorated, the walls cleaned, and replicas of the original bronze chandelier and sconces installed. Heavy scarlet brocade draperies, reproductions of the originals, were hung in the old visitors' gallery. Duplicates of the original fireplace mantels and two ornately carved frames holding engraved copies of the Declaration of Independence were also placed in the Chamber.

Much of the Capitol's greatest interior decorative art was completed during a twenty-five year period by Constantino Brumidi, a talented painter and muralist who fled political persecution in his native Italy, arriving in the United States in 1852. In 1855 he began the embellishment of the United States Capitol; his legacy includes the corridors of the Senate Wing, the formal offices of the President and Vice President, the Senate Reception Room, the present House and Senate Appropriations Committee's rooms, and most important, his work in the Rotunda. In 1877, when he was seventy-two years old, Brumidi began his last work, the fresco

The original House of Representatives Chamber was restored to some of its 1822 splendor during 1976. The Chamber became Statuary Hall in 1864.

Originally, a grand staircase occupied this space. After the fire of 1814, Latrobe abandoned that design and constructed a small rotunda inside the existing oval space.

Every day the Rotunda fills with thousands of visitors interested in the art and history of the building.

frieze encircling the top of the Rotunda. Its subjects include various epic events in American history, such as the landing of Columbus, William Penn's treaty with the Indians, the great battles of the Revolution, and the discovery of gold in California. Brumidi had completed about one quarter of the work when his scaffold slipped. He managed to save himself by clinging onto the platform for 20 minutes until help came, but the shock was so great that he was never able to return to his work. He died four months later in February 1880. During the following eight years, Filippo Costaggini completed the great frieze using Brumidi's cartoons, except for a thirty-two foot gap that was

Prayer Room for Members of Congress.

completed by Allyn Cox in 1953. Brumidi's great wish, which he once expressed in a letter, was "that I may live long enough to make beautiful the Capitol of the one country on earth in which there is liberty". Every visitor to the Capitol sees the evidence of his success.

Throughout the latter half of the century, numerous conveniences were installed in the Capitol. Plumbing, steam heat, and forced air ventilation were introduced by 1865; the first elevators went into operation in 1874; the building was more adequately fireproofed in 1881; and by 1900 the Capitol was completely wired for electricity. The engineers in charge of planning the new plumbing system were appalled at the condition of the old water closet drains: they claimed the build-up of sewer gas was so great that a single spark could have touched off a massive explosion. As a by-product of the modernization process, the Capitol did lose some of its romance; one by one its fireplaces were walled up or removed, until now there are few that are operable. The chimneys remain, however: there are no fewer than one hundred and thirty-nine on the roof.

The walls of Senate corridors are part of an elaborate decorative scheme developed and executed by Constantino Brumidi.

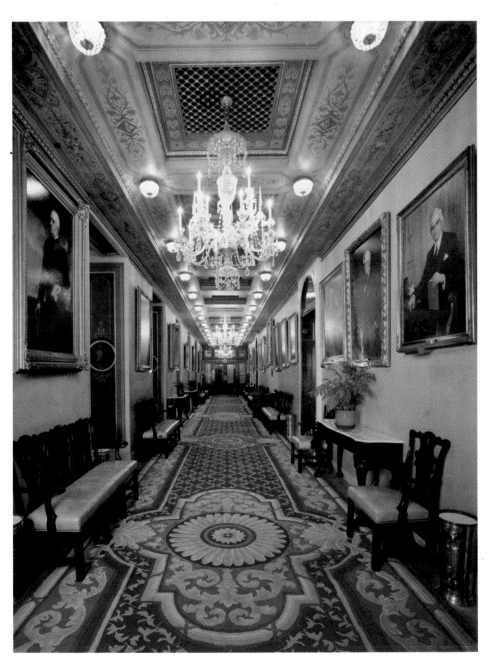

The Speaker's Lobby is located behind the House of Representatives Chamber. After a Speaker of the House retires, his portrait is hung in this area of the Capitol.

Capitol Landscape and Improvements

The West Front of the Capitol once overlooked marshland, a canal and a railroad station. The Olmsted grounds (1880's) and the design of the Mall (early 20th century) provided the green areas known today.

During the years 1865 through 1900, the Capitol's natural surroundings began to acquire the grace and dignity they retain today. When the Capitol was built, the Grounds were planted in a rural, informal manner. One writer described the soil at that time as being "exceedingly stiff clay, becoming dust in dry and mortar in rainy weather". Only four decades later, however, Mrs. Trollope, the English chronicler, called the Grounds an "exceedingly handsome enclosure", and accurately predicted that "in a few years, [they] will offer the shade of all the most splendid trees which flourish in the Union". Today, after several annexations, they comprise a remarkable green oasis in the city.

Tourists enjoy them, and Congressional employees relax under the great trees during their lunch hours. The Capitol Grounds comprise 181 acres today, and contain more than one hundred species of plants, shrubs, and trees, including the symbolic gifts of State trees from thirty-three States of the Union. The native species of the Eastern United States predominate, with nine varieties of maple and elm, and twelve of oak; also planted on the Grounds is a giant sequoia, the king of trees, a gift of the State of California.

Not until 1874 were the Capitol Grounds embellished by the master landscaper whose work is still abundantly evident to us today. Frederick Law Olmsted, the greatest landscape

This print from a drawing by Hughson Hawley was done around the turn of the century. It shows the new Olmsted terraces and an Edward Clark proposal for the construction of a pediment and large portico on the West Front.

Tulips in bloom on the West Front of the Capitol.

Frederick L. Olmsted was hired by the Senate Committee on Buildings and Grounds in 1874 to landscape the Capitol campus. This master plan also shows an extension on the Capitol to the West that was being planned concurrently.

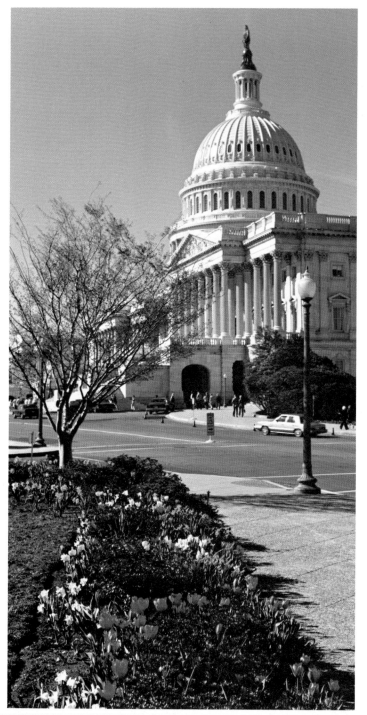

Tulips among azaleas on the Capitol plaza.

architect in America, came to Washington fresh from his triumph in New York City, where he planned Central Park. Arriving in the Federal City, he remarked that the Capitol Grounds were in a state of "sylvan juvenility", and he immediately set to work planning the graceful plantings and walks that have delighted visitors ever since. Mr. Olmsted recognized that the soil of the Capitol Grounds was too impoverished to support the extensive plantings he recommended, so his first task was to improve its fertility. His work crews plowed and drained the soil, dressed it with oyster-shell lime and swamp muck, exposed the mix to a winter's frosts, and then topped it all off with a compost of manure and more swamp muck, a necessary process, but one which also must surely have brought a pungent aroma to Capitol Hill during the warm summer months. Olmsted's plans were warmly received by Congress, but on one occasion he found his grand scheme supplanted by the desires of the Senate. One morning in 1875, Senator Simon Cameron of Pennsylvania was crossing the Grounds on his way to the Capitol when he saw a work crew preparing to chop down an ancient and majestic elm near the House which stood in the way of one of Mr. Olmsted's proposed promenades. Senator Cameron demanded that the workmen stop, and then ran to the Senate Chamber, where his fellow Members had already begun their session. Begging the floor from the Senator who was speaking at the time, he

Crabapple trees on the Senate side.

rose and asked the Senate to express its opinion that the handsome and venerable elm ought to be spared. The tree flourishes today near the House entrance; it has, in fact, been named the "Cameron Elm" in honor of its savior.

Olmsted's work at the Capitol was not confined to landscaping. He was also responsible for the design of a very prominent part of the Capitol's structure: the graceful and dignified West Front terraces which replaced Bulfinch's earthen terraces of 1829. He also designed and erected a rocky grotto on the Senate side of the Grounds with spring water piped in from the northern section of the city; it has served as a shady retreat for generations of visitors. Yet even as Olmsted proceeded with his work, there were occasional reminders that elegant landscaping and terraces could not change the fact that Washington was still a small city. A routine report filed in 1877, at the height of Mr. Olmsted's activity, recommended that Congress make a special appropriation to replace tender shrubbery and young trees damaged by the cattle that wandered onto the Capitol Grounds.

Early in the twentieth century, the Capitol was joined on the summit of Capitol Hill by two office buildings, one for each House. The Capitol had become uncomfortably overcrowded, and the two new structures were needed to accommodate a Congress grown to four hundred and thirty-five Representatives and ninety-six Senators. The House office building was later named for the late Speaker Joseph Cannon, and that of the Senate for the late Senator Richard Russell of Georgia.

Two additional House office buildings, named for the late Speakers Nicholas Longworth of Ohio and Sam Rayburn of Texas, as well as a second building for the Senate, named for the late Senator Everett Dirksen of Illinois, have also been constructed.

Longworth House Office Building.

Cannon House Office Building.

Rayburn House Office Building.

Russell Senate Office Building.

Dirksen Senate Office Building.

Thomas U. Walter's plans (1865) for the extension of the East Front of the Capitol were realized about 100 years later. The Architect of the Capitol, J. George Stewart, directed this complex project.

Improvements within the Capitol Building itself have also continued throughout this century. In 1929, Congress authorized the installation of air conditioning, then a radical innovation, in the Capitol and the House and Senate Office Buildings. When the Capitol Power Plant was completed three years later, it was the largest air conditioning unit in the world. The year 1958 saw the beginning of construction on the largest modification made to the Capitol since Thomas Walter's dome was finished in 1863. Over the years, the aging sandstone East Front of the Capitol had seriously deteriorated. During the following four years a new front, duplicating the old front but extending it by thirty-two feet, was constructed from marble; this new addition provided space for offices and public rooms. The extension was a fulfillment of the intention of Walter's original plans of 1874. From the time he designed the House and Senate wings in the 1850s, he had urged for the sake of proportion that the East Front be extended.

Visitors to the Capitol in the Bicentennial Year found the building more

Gardens above the House garage.

beautiful than ever; the interior was cleaned and repainted, and the Old Supreme Court, Senate Chamber, and Statuary Hall were restored. In the ground floor of the House Wing, artist Allyn Cox finished a spectacular series of murals depicting the many meeting places of Congress and great moments in the history of the Capitol. The project must have seemed like a nostalgic homecoming to Mr. Cox; he had worked in the Capitol once before, in the 1950s, when he completed Constantino Brumidi's Rotunda frieze.

Repairs to sidewalk on the East Front of Capitol.

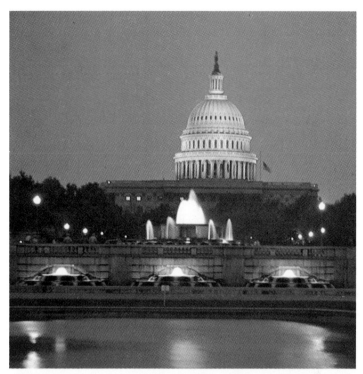

The Capitol from Senate side.

Tulip time at the Capitol.

Artist Allyn Cox (seated) with Representative Augustus F. Hawkins of California, Chairman, Committee on House Administration (standing far left); Senator Charles McC. Mathias, Jr., of Maryland, Chairman, Senate Committee on Rules and Administration (standing right) and George M. White, Architect of the Capitol (kneeling). The painting of the signing of the Declaration of Independence is in the corridor of the House Wing.

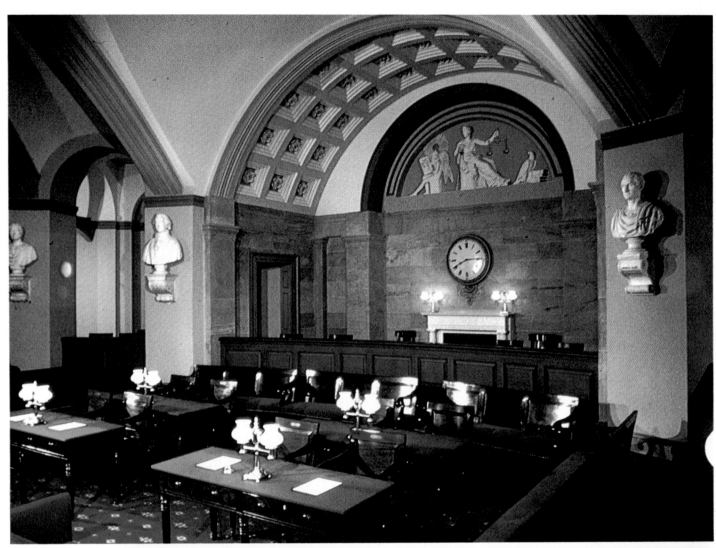

The Old Supreme
Court Chamber was
restored to include
reproductions of
furnishings used in the
Chamber in the 1800s.
This project, directed
by George M. White,
Architect of the
Capitol, was completed
in 1976.

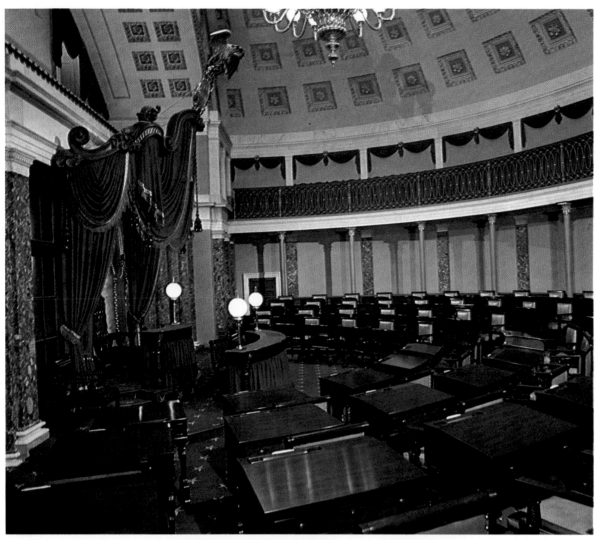

Restoration of the old Senate Chamber was completed in June of 1976 under the supervision of the Senate Commission on Art and Antiquities. The mid-nineteenth century furnishings remind one of the days of the eloquence of Webster, Clay and Calhoun.

"The United States Senate, A.D. 1850," engraved by Robert Whitechurch after Peter Rothermel. Henry Clay presents his program of compromise in the Old Senate Chamber, presided over by Vice President Millard Fillmore. John C. Calhoun appears to the right of the Vice President and Daniel Webster is seated left foreground, head in hand.

Second floor passageway after modification. Caen stone walls, octagonal marble floor, ornamental plaster ceiling and appropriate chandelier embellish the space.

Second floor passageway before reconstruction. The passage was constructed in 1901. At that time, the walls were covered in white glazed brick.

The dramatic design of Benjamin H. Latrobe, Second Architect of the Capitol, is captured in this award winning extreme wide angle photograph of this stairwell on the Senate side of the Capitol. Latrobe planned this powerful, elegant and essential staircase after the catastrophic fire of 1814. Photograph by Harry L. Burnett, Jr., of the Architect's Office.

Memorial and Historic Trees
on the United States Capitol Grounds

Since the early 1900s, ninety-four memorial and historic trees have been planted. Seventy-three are still living on the Capitol Grounds—this chart and guide will help to locate them.

(a) Memorial or historic tree which has been removed from the Capitol Grounds.
(b) Memorial or historic tree located in the courtyard to the Everett McKinley Dirksen Office Building.
(c) Memorial or historic trees located in the lower West Court Terrace of the Rayburn House Office Building.
(d) Russell Courtyard.

Key No.	Date planted	Planted by or memorializing	State	Common name of tree	Botanical name of tree
(a)	Prior to 1800	George Washington	Virginia	American Elm	*Ulmus americana.*
38	Prior to 1875	Senator Simon D. Cameron	Pennsylvania	American Elm	*Ulmus americana.*
(a)	April 18, 1912	Vice President James S. Sherman	New York	Purple Beech	*Fagus sylvatica.*
(a)	April 24, 1912	Senator Augustus O. Bacon	Georgia	Pin Oak	*Quercus palustris.*
44	April 24, 1912	Representative William J. Browning	New Jersey	Red Oak	*Quercus borealis.*
2	April 30, 1912	Senator Jacob H. Gallinger	New Hampshire	Overcup Oak	*Quercus lyrata.*
(a)	May 4, 1912	Senator Henry C. Lodge, Sr.	Massachusetts	Red Oak	*Quercus borealis.*
18	May 4, 1912	Representative James R. Mann	Illinois	Red Oak	*Quercus borealis.*
19	May 7, 1912	Speaker Champ Clark	Missouri	Sugar Maple	*Acer saccharum.*
4	May 9, 1912	Senator Shelby M. Cullom	Illinois	American Elm	*Ulmus americana.*
(a)	May 11, 1912	Senator George P. Wetmore	Rhode Island	American Beech	*Fagus americana.*
(a)	April 21, 1913	Representative Richard Bartholdt (Peace Tree)	Missouri	Pin Oak	*Quercus palustris.*
41	1913	Representative Marlin E. Olmsted	Pennsylvania	Pin Oak	*Quercus palustris.*
34	1913	Speaker Joseph G. Cannon	Illinois	Red Oak	*Quercus borealis.*
33	1916 or 1917	Representative Joseph Taggart	Kansas	Pin Oak	*Quercus palustris.*

Key No.	Date planted	Planted by or memorializing	State	Common name of tree	Botanical name of tree
(a)	1917 or 1918	Representative Jeannette Rankin	Montana	Redwood	*Sequoia gigantea.*
8	April 8, 1918	Vice President Thomas R. Marshall	Indiana	Hickory	*Hicoria alba.*
13	April 8, 1918	Senator Willard Saulsbury	Delaware	Hickory	*Hicoria alba.*
(a)	1918 or 1919	Representative James L. Slayden	Texas	Pecan	*Hicoria pecan.*
42	1918 or 1919	Representative James L. Slayden	Texas	Pecan	*Hicoria pecan.*
39	1920	Representative Charles H. Randall	California	Redwood	*Sequoia gigantea.*
17	April 15, 1920	Representative Joseph Walsh	Massachusetts	American Beech	*Fagus grandiflora.*
(a)	April 20, 1923	Senator Charles L. McNary	Oregon	Red Oak	*Quercus borealis.*
(a)	May 9, 1925	Mothers' Tree (planted to honor Mothers of America)	All States	White Birch	*Betula laciniata.*
(a)	Nov. 23, 1927	Representative Martin B. Madden	Illinois	Mossycup Oak	*Quercus macrocarpa.*
40	Nov. 26, 1927	Representative David H. Kincheloe	Kentucky	Umbrella Tree	*Magnolia tripetala.*
(a)	May 4, 1928	Representative Roy G. Fitzgerald	Ohio	Bullbay Tree	*Magnolia grandiflora.*
(a)	1929–1933	Vice President Charles Curtis	Kansas	Bullbay Tree	*Magnolia grandiflora.*
(a)	May 1929	Senator Simeon D. Fess	Ohio	Buckeye	*Aesculus glabra.*
(a)	April 20, 1931	Boy Scout Tree (from Mount Vernon, Va.) First step in nut tree planting program	Virginia	White Walnut	*Juglans cinerea.*
(a)	Dec. 21, 1931	Scion of Washington Elm (from Washington State)	Washington	American Elm	*Ulmus americana.*
(a)	Dec. 21, 1931	Representative Maurice H. Thatcher	Kentucky	American Elm	*Ulmus americana.*
28	April 22, 1932	To honor 100th anniversary of the birth of J. Sterling Morton, founder of Arbor Day; and bicentennial of George Washington	Virginia	Black Walnut	*Juglans nigra.*
30	April 8, 1936	J. Sterling Morton Tree (Representative Karl Stefan, sponsor)	Nebraska	White Pine	*Pinus strobus.*
(a)	Nov. 9, 1939	Sam Houston Centennial Tree (replanted by Fritz G. Lanham)	Texas	Pecan	*Hicoria pecan.*
15	May 30, 1946	War Memorial Tree (Representative John E. Rankin, sponsor)	All States	White Oak	*Quercus alba.*
6	April 10, 1947	Arbor Day Tree—75th anniversary of Arbor Day (Senator Kenneth Wherry, sponsor)	Nebraska	Burr Oak	*Quercus macrocarpa.*
27	June 26, 1948	Good Templars Tree (plaque placed on existing tree)		American Elm	*Ulmus americana.*
14	April 16, 1949	Memorial to Senator Thomas P. Gore	Oklahoma	Chestnut Oak	*Quercus prinus.*
49	April 16, 1949	Memorial to Senator Robert L. Owen	Oklahoma	Sweet Gum	*Liquidamber styraciflua.*
35	Oct. 11, 1949	Speaker Sam Rayburn	Texas	White Oak	*Quercus alba.*
32	Sept. 2, 1950	Memorial to Representative Chester C. Bolton	Ohio	Buckeye	*Aesculus glabra.*
11	Nov. 16, 1951	Greater North Dakota Association	North Dakota	American Elm	*Ulmus americana.*
16	June 12, 1952	Memorial to 5 Sullivan Brothers killed in World War II	Iowa	5 Crab Apples	*Pyrus malus.*

Cameron Elm, circa 1920.

Vice President James S. Sherman planting a tree on the Senate side of the Capitol on April 18, 1912.

(a) Memorial or historic tree which has been removed from the Capitol Grounds.
(b) Memorial or historic tree located in the courtyard to the Everett McKinley Dirksen Office Building.
(c) Memorial or historic trees located in the lower West Court Terrace of the Rayburn House Office Building.
(d) Russell Courtyard.

Key No.	Date planted	Planted by or memorializing	State	Common name of tree	Botanical name of tree
5	April 28, 1954	Senator Leverett Saltonstall	Massachusetts	Red Maple	Acer rubrum.
25	July 8, 1954	Speaker Joseph W. Martin, Jr.	Massachusetts	English Elm	Ulmus Procera.
26	May 17, 1955	Michigan State Society	Michigan	White Pine	Pinus strobus.
1	Nov. 13, 1963	State of Georgia (Senator Richard B. Russell, sponsor)	Georgia	Loblolly Pine	Pinus taeda.
29	Nov. 18, 1963	Representative Carl Vinson	Georgia	White Oak	Quercus alba.
21	Nov. 18, 1963	Representative James C. Auchincloss	New Jersey	Red Oak	Quercus borealis.
45	May 13, 1964	Boys' Clubs of America	All States	Red Pine	Pinus resinosa.
36	June 11, 1964	Speaker John W. McCormack	Massachusetts	Sugar Maple	Acer saccharum.
23	June 11, 1964	Representative Charles A. Halleck	Indiana	Yellow poplar	Liriodendron tulipifera.
43	March 17, 1965	Potomac Area Council of Camp Fire Girls (commemorating Founders Day)	District of Columbia	Saucer Magnolia	Magnolia soulangeania.
3	April 6, 1965	State Society of New Jersey (Senator Clifford P. Case, sponsor)	New Jersey	Northern Red Oak	Quercus borealis.
47	May 3, 1965	Senator Jack Miller	Iowa	Black Walnut	Juglans nigra.
46	May 20, 1965	Memorial to Senator Robert S. Kerr	Oklahoma	Redbud	Cercis canadensis.
(d)	May 26, 1965	State of New Jersey (Senator Harrison A. Williams, Jr., sponsor)	New Jersey	Red Oak	Quercus borealis.
7	March 29, 1966	Congressional Women's Club (Senators' Wives)		Deodar Cedar	Cedrus deodara.
31	March 29, 1966	Congressional Women's Club (Representatives' Wives)		Deodar Cedar	Cedrus deodara.
48	May 25, 1966	Cherokee Indian Nation (commemorating 200th anniversary of birth of Sequoyah)	Georgia	Redwood	Sequoia gigantea.
22	April 3, 1967	State of Ohio (Representative Clarence E. Miller, sponsor)	Ohio	Buckeye	Aesculus glabra.
10	April 16, 1967	Arbor Lodge Association of Nebraska City, Nebr. (Senator Carl T. Curtis, sponsor)	Nebraska	Maidenhair	Ginkgo biloba.
37	April 28, 1967	Washington Township of New Jersey (Representative John E. Hunt, sponsor)	New Jersey	Cherry Tree	Prunus Mount Fuji.
(b)	May 4, 1967	Mrs. Lyndon B. Johnson		Redbud	Cercis canadensis.
12	April 30, 1968	Mrs. Lyndon B. Johnson (Senate Wives, sponsors)		Chinese Dogwood	Cornus kousa.
24	May 1, 1969	In Commemoration of the Centennial of Blair, Nebr. (Representative Glenn Cunningham, sponsor)	Nebraska	Blair Maple	Acer saccarinum Blairi.
9	June 4, 1969	State of Illinois (dedicated to and planted by Senator Everett M. Dirksen)	Illinois	Pin Oak	Quercus palustris.
52	April 14, 1970	State of Tennessee (Representative Richard H. Fulton)	Tennessee	Tulip Poplar	Liriodendron tulipifera.
50	Oct. 25, 1971	The Jewish Campaign for the People's Peace Treaty		Bradford Callery Pear	Pyrus Calleryana Bradford.

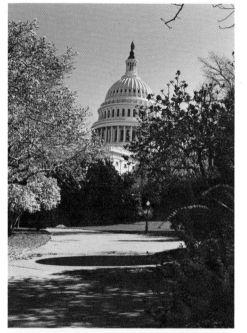

Tulip Magnolia and
Cherry Trees on the
Capitol Grounds.

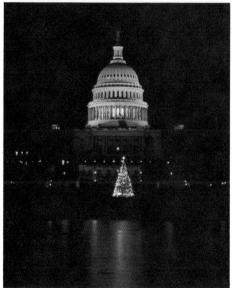

U.S. Capitol Christmas
Tree. Photograph
by Senator
Howard H. Baker, Jr.,
of Tennessee.

Key No.	Date planted	Planted by or memorializing	State	Common name of tree	Botanical name of tree
51	April 28, 1972	Commemoration of the 100th Anniversary of the First Arbor Day Observance		Japanese Zelkova	*Zelkova serrata.*
54	April 2, 1973	State of Wisconsin (Senator Gaylord Nelson)	Wisconsin	Sugar Maple	*Acer saccharum.*
53	April 10, 1973	The Senate Ladies Gift to Mrs. Richard M. Nixon		Southern Magnolia	*Magnolia grandiflora.*
55	Sept. 26, 1974	In Honor of his Retirement, Representative Dave Martin	Nebraska	American Elm	*Ulmus americana.*
56	Nov. 22, 1974	In Honor of his Retirement, Senator Sam J. Ervin, Jr.	North Carolina	White Dogwood	*Cornus florida.*
57	Dec. 19, 1974	State of Washington (Senator Henry M. Jackson)	Washington	Douglas Fir	*Pseudotsuga taxifolia.*
58	June 10, 1975	Idaho Federation of Women's Clubs (planted by Senator James A. McClure)	Idaho	White Pine	*Pinus strobus.*
59	March 12, 1976	In Commemoration of birthdate of Juliet Gordon Lowe (Girl Scout Council of the National Capitol Area)		Sassafras	*Sassafras albidum.*
60	April 5, 1976	State of Maryland (Senator J. Glenn Beall, Jr.)	Maryland	Wye Oak seedling	*Quercus alba var. wye.*
61	April 27, 1976	In Honor of his Retirement, Senator Roman L. Hruska	Nebraska	Bradford Pear	*Pyrus Calleryana Bradford.*
62	April 29, 1976	Michigan State Society (Senator Philip A. Hart)	Michigan	American Spruce, Red, White & Blue	*Picea Hybrid.*
63	May 5, 1976	American Mothers Committee, Inc., Honoring Mothers of America		Crapemyrtle	*Lagerstroemia indica.*
64	May 6, 1976	Arbor Day Delegation from Nebraska	Nebraska	Cottonwood	*Populus deltoides.*
65	July 7, 1976	Tulare County American Revolution Bi-Centennial Commission (Plano 4-H Bi-Centennial Flag Corps and Porterville High School Choir)	California	Redwood	*Sequoia gigantea.*
66	Nov. 22, 1976	Citizens of Paw Paw, West Virginia	West Virginia	Paw Paw	*Asimina trioba.*
67	Dec. 9, 1976	In Honor of his Retirement, Speaker Carl Albert		Redbud	*Cercis canadensis.*
68	April 29, 1977	National Arbor Day (Representative Hamilton Fish, Senator Jacob K. Javits and Representative Frederick W. Richmond)		Hybrid Elm	*Ulmus Sapporo Autumn Gold.*
69	June 6, 1977	1977 Graduation Class (House of Representatives Page School)		Mountain Ash	*Sorbus aucuparia.*
70	March 15, 1978	Members of the Texas Delegation, 95th Congress	Texas	Hybrid Pecan	*Carya ill. var. Kiowa.*
71	March 27, 1978	Liberty Tree seedling (Senator Charles McC. Mathias)	Maryland	Tulip Poplar	*Liriodendron tulipfera.*
(c)	May 25, 1978	Republican Congressional Wives Honoring Mrs. Richard Nixon and Mrs. Gerald Ford (Mrs. Gerald Ford)		Golden-chain	*Laburnum anagyroides.*
72	June 12, 1978	1978 Graduation Class (House of Representatives Page School)		Mountain Ash	*Sorbus aucuparia.*
73	Oct. 5, 1978	California State Society (Representative Fortney H. Stark, Jr.)	California	Redwood	*Sequoia gigantea.*
74	March 23, 1979	In Honor of his Retirement, Representative Olin E. Teague		Bradford Pear	*Pyrus Calleryana Bradford.*
75	June 11, 1979	1979 Graduation Class (House of Representatives Page School)		Japanese Pagoda	*Sophora Japonica.*

Botanic Garden

The United States Botanic Garden was founded in 1820 under the auspices of the Columbia Institute for the Promotion of Arts and Sciences, an outgrowth of an association known as the Metropolitan Society, which received its charter from Congress on April 20, 1818. The Botanic Garden continued under the direction of this Institute until 1837, when the Institute ceased to exist as an active organization.

The Botanic Garden thereafter remained abandoned until 1842, when it became necessary for the Government to provide accommodations for the botanical collections brought to Washington, D.C., from the South Seas by the U.S. Exploring Expedition of 1838–1842, under the leadership of Captain Charles Wilkes. The collection was temporarily placed on exhibition on a lot behind the Patent Office building. A greenhouse was constructed under the direction and control of Congress' Joint Committee on the Li-

brary. Upon completion of the greenhouse, the collection from the exploring expedition was placed therein and was put under the custodianship of the Commissioner of Patents by the Library Committee. The actual care of the botanical collections was under the supervision of Captain Wilkes, assisted by William D. Brackenridge, a horticulturist and assistant botanist for the expedition.

In 1849 Congress authorized the construction of an extension to the Patent Office building, making it necessary to relocate the Botanic Garden greenhouses annexed thereto. The site selected by the Joint Committee on the Library for the relocation was at the west end of the Capitol Grounds, practically the same location as that occupied by the Botanic Garden during the period it functioned under the Columbia Institute. The construction of a new greenhouse on this site was placed under the supervision of

United States Botanic Garden.

the Architect of the Capitol, with the approval of the Joint Committee on the Library.

For many years following this relocation, there existed an intention to secure for the Botanic Garden more adequate facilities for carrying on its work, to place it on a level with other botanic gardens throughout the country.

On January 7, 1925, Congress took definite steps toward this goal by authorizing the preparation of preliminary plans, and later approved the project by authorization of funds for the site, for the construction of new conservatories and other necessary buildings and for the relocation of the Bartholdi fountain.

The Bartholdi fountain was originally exhibited at the 1876 International Exhibition held in Philadelphia, and had been purchased by the U.S. Government in 1877 for six thousand dollars. The architect of the fountain was Frederic Auguste Bartholdi, a French sculptor who also designed the Statue of Liberty.

The fountain is constructed of bronzed iron, cast in Paris by A. Dureene. The entire structure is thirty feet high, and rests in the center of a large marble basin, supported by a triangular pedestal, on the faces of which are aquatic reptiles and fishes spouting water. Upon this pedestal stand three female caryatids supporting another basin, from the rim of which twelve Victorian lamps are suspended gracefully. The fountain is surmounted by a crown, through which the water flows.

Spring flower show.

Interior of the Conservatory.

Bartholdi Fountain.

39

Flowering cactus.

The cornerstone of the new conservatory was laid on November 12, 1931; the new buildings were occupied on January 13, 1933.

Structurally, the design of the new conservatory follows conventional form, with an arched and domed roof frame carrying the great expanse of glass sheathing. In its details the design presents many points of interest, among which is the extensive use of aluminum for structural members—the first time aluminum had been used for such purposes. The main feature is the one-story loggia or entrance hall forming the Maryland Avenue front. It is built of limestone, carried to a height of about 40 feet and has a series of lofty arched doorways. The main conservatory is approximately 262 feet in length and 183 feet in width.

The square across Independence Avenue south of the Conservatory was developed as an outdoor garden—this is the site of the relocated Bartholdi fountain. The Botanic Garden property also includes more than 22 acres known as Poplar Point Nursery, adjacent to Anacostia Park. This property was added to the United States Botanic Garden in 1926.

Interior orchid collection.

Chrysanthemum show.

Christmas at the
Botanic Garden.

Interior courtyard of
Botanic Garden in the
springtime.

41

Art in the Capitol

The Capitol itself can be considered a work of art. The classical architecture and the interior embellishments from Latrobe's corn cob capitals to Brumidi's powerful dome painting provide a beautiful ambience. A complete survey of the various paintings, sculptures, and decorative details found in the Capitol is available in the catalog, *Art in the U.S. Capitol* (House Document 94–660), prepared by the Architect of the Capitol under the direction of the Joint Committee on the Library.

The following pages provide only a few examples of the artistic treasures found in the Capitol.

Brumidi's dome and frieze paintings complement the classical cast iron details of Thomas Walter's dome. A bronze replica of Houdon's statue of George Washington stands in the foreground.

Benjamin Latrobe designed the corn cob capitals for the columns in the foyer outside the Old Supreme Court Chamber (1809).

Some of Brumidi's most beautiful room paintings are found in S–127, the Senate Committee on Appropriations' room. Pompeian architecture and allegorical figures dominate the compositions on all the walls and ceiling.

On the first floor of the Senate corridor Brumidi painted walls and ceilings with medallion portraits, sketches of major inventions, and paintings of birds, animals and flowers.

The ceiling in the President's Room is ornately decorated. This allegoric female figure is reminiscent of earlier Italian paintings of Madonnas.

The President's Room,
with frescoes and oil
paintings, dates to
about 1860. Until the
1930s Presidents
signed bills at the
mahogany table under
the great crystal
chandelier.

"Washington at Valley Forge, 1778" is on the south wall of the Senate Appropriations' room.

"Scene at the Signing of the Constitution", by Howard Chandler Christy, was commissioned by Congress in 1940 for the east stairway of the House Wing. This 20 x 30 foot canvas, largest in the Capitol, is remarkable for its historic detail and its patriotic inspiration. Eleven years after independence was declared, the leaders of the new nation met in Independence Hall, September 17, 1787 to place their names on this modern document of freedom. Well known likenesses of George Washington, Benjamin Franklin, Alexander Hamilton, and James Madison are easily recognized.

"First Reading of the Emancipation Proclamation", by Francis B. Carpenter, in west staircase of Senate Wing. Lincoln is shown with his cabinet. Seated: Edwin M. Stanton, President Lincoln, Gideon Welles, William H. Seward, Edward Bates; standing: Salmon P. Chase, Caleb B. Smith, Montgomery Blair.

"Calling of Putnam From the Plow to the Revolution" is on the west wall of the House Appropriations' room. Putnam left his farm to fight in the Battle of Breed's Hill, June 16, 1775.

"The Declaration of Independence", one of the eight paintings in the Rotunda, depicts a monumental event in our history in Independence Hall, Philadelphia, July 4, 1776. The 56 signers, all members of the Continental Congress, risked death to tell the world that "for the support of this Declaration . . . we mutually pledge to each other our Lives, our Fortunes, and our sacred Honor".

"George Washington" by Rembrandt Peale. This distinguished portrait is known because of its illusionistically painted frame as the "porthole portrait." Purchased for the Senate in 1832, it hangs in the Old Senate Chamber.

Diagram of bronze
doors of the main
entrance to Rotunda—
East Front United
States Capitol.

The Columbus Doors,
designed by Randolph
Rogers, originally
hung in the corridor
connecting Statuary
Hall with the House
Wing. In 1871 they
were moved to the
East Front entrance.

Inside the Capitol dome. Constantino Brumidi's "Apotheosis of Washington", the fresco in the canopy of the dome, is a masterful allegorical work of art. Brumidi worked 11 months painting this masterpiece; he signed it in 1865. The 13 original colonies surround Washington, who is flanked by Liberty and Victory and Fame. Other allegorical figures averaging 25 feet in height symbolize the Arts and Sciences, the Sea, Commerce, Mechanics, Agriculture, War and Freedom.

"C. Brumidi, Artist, Citizen of the U.S." is how Brumidi signed "Cornwallis Sues for Cessation of Hostilities Under the Flag of Truce". The fresco, once in the House of Representatives is now in the House Dining Room.

1

Gods and mortals mingle in the Dome's fresco. (1) Ceres rides a reaper as Young America, wearing a liberty cap, stands near. (2) Vulcan rests his foot on a cannon. (3) Bearded Neptune and Aphrodite, holding the Atlantic cable, rise from the sea. (4) Sandaled Mercury offers a bag of gold to Robert Morris, "Financier of the Revolution." (5) Wise Minerva speaks to Benjamin Franklin, S. F. B. Morse, and Robert Fulton. (6) Armed Freedom—Brumidi's young wife was the model—triumphs over Tyranny and Kingly Power.

2

3

4

5

6

Lawgivers Who Advanced the March to Human Freedom

*The Laws of Old
and of Today
Seek to Glorify
the Dignity of Man*

Location of the 23
Marble Relief Portraits
Over the Gallery
Doors, House of
Representatives.

The United States Congress today has awesome, world-wide responsibilities. One of its little-reflected-upon tasks, however, is one of its most important. The Congress today must pick up the mantle of a centuries-old struggle: to develop and improve upon a workable, enforceable, and equitable system of justice.

The founding fathers performed a remarkable feat during that long hot Philadelphia summer in 1789. They did not, however, start from scratch. They drew upon the knowledge and wisdom, and the failures, of three thousand years of recorded history. Any visitor to the House Chamber will appreciate the fact that our modern law-makers are building upon a priceless heritage of Western civilization.

As a constant reminder of its task, the Congress directed that the upper walls of the House Chamber be adorned with 23 marble relief portraits of noted "Lawgivers". Created in bas relief on white Vermont marble, by seven different sculptors, the plaques each measure 28" in diameter. One is full face; the other 22 are profiles. From the full face of Moses on the north wall, 11 profiles face left and 11 face right, ending at a quotation from Daniel Webster on the south wall above the Speaker's chair.

The subjects of the plaques were jointly chosen by a group from the University of Pennsylvania and the Columbia Historical Society of Washington, D.C., in consultation with expert staff from the Library of Congress. The selection was approved by a special committee of five Members of the House of Representatives, the Architect of the Capitol, and his associates.

The struggle for an effective and equitable system of justice has been slow and uncertain. The world has suffered far more often under the yoke of despots than it has prospered under a rule of law. In fact, even in the histories of some of the celebrated lawgivers displayed in the House Chamber, lives of despotism and ruthlessness mix with noble resolve and high motive. However, taken in the context of their times, their individual contributions served to advance the rule of law. As a free people, we do right to honor their contributions.

Hammurabi

2067–2025 B.C., the Babylonian king and lawgiver. More than seventeen hundred years before Christ—according to the latest chronology—he gave to his age and to mankind, the code of laws that bears his name. Historically one of the first four lawgivers known to civilization, he ruled his people justly—"that the strong shall not oppress the weak"—and through law gave his people contentment and prosperity.

Moses

1571–1451 B.C., the Hebrew lawgiver and prophet, thundered the Ten Commandments from Mount Sinai more than three thousand years ago. He was the great administrator who created a nation, cementing law with religion, and giving to the ages a tough moral code that is the foundation for the noblest ideas of man on the dignity of the individual.

Lycurgus

Lawgiver of Sparta who reformed its constitution about the seventh or ninth century B.C. He established a more equitable basis for the ownership of property and is said to have enacted laws so sound they remained in force nearly a thousand years.

Solon

638–558 B.C., Athenian statesman, businessman and legislator, known as one of the Seven Wise Men of Greece, who may be said to have pioneered a form of democratic government by cutting down the unlimited powers of the nobility. Citizens were granted juries to act as courts of last instance. Under the great new law code he erected, contracts were illegal that bartered a man's liberty.

Gaius

110–180, Roman jurist whose most important work, *Institutes,* a popular manual of Roman law, was incorporated almost bodily in the widely known *Institutes of Justinian.* He flourished around the second century of the Christian era, giving us what many believe is the first elementary textbook on the law in the modern sense.

Papinian

About 200 A.D., a strict moralist, he is regarded among the greatest of the Roman jurists.

Justinian I

483–565, Byzantine Emperor, made his contribution as a legislator and a jurist, giving the world the Code of Justinian, compiled by a commission of lawyers he appointed. This *Corpus Juris Civilis* is said to constitute the nucleus of nearly all modern European systems, and to have influenced the common law of England.

Tribonian

500–547, was Justinian's top law officer. Law editor and director of the compilation of Justinian's *Corpus Juris Civilis,* he gave to posterity the benefit of his vast technical knowledge of Roman Law.

Maimonides

1135–1204, rabbi, physician, law-codifier, profoundly influenced non-Jewish as well as Jewish thought, with his monumental work organizing and systematizing Jewish oral law. Widely known also is his *Guide For The Perplexed* which has been translated into English.

Gregory IX

1147–1241, Pope, promulgated an impressive compilation of decretals—a collection of decrees—as a standard textbook in canon law.

Innocent III

Pope, 1161–1216, active and diligent as a judge, respected for his judicial impartiality, stands as one of the foremost figures of medieval times.

de Montfort

1200–65, championed the cause of the nobles and the people against the king—thereby establishing a precedent—and created a place for himself in history by calling the Great Parliament which brought together for this assembly representatives from towns and boroughs.

St. Louis

1214–70, King of France (Louis IX), canonized in 1297. His rule was marked by justice and competence and he has been characterized as the ideal king of the Middle Ages. Author of *Mise of Amiens.*

Alphonso X

1221–84, Spanish King and patron of learning, is credited with doing much for *Las Siete Partidas,* a compilation of Roman and canon law.

Edward I

1239–1307, King of England, sometimes called the English Justinian. He compiled the *Statutes of Westminster,* influenced striking developments in law and espoused constitutional principles.

Suleiman I

1494–1566, Sultan of the Turkish Empire. Distinguished in Turkish history as The Lawyer and in European history as The Magnificent, he improved the status of Christians in his domains, and set up a new and better system of laws to govern an empire he widely extended. He won himself immortality as a legislator.

Grotius

1583–1645, Dutch jurist and humanist. His *De jure qelli et pacis* has been called "one of the greatest masterpieces of legal literature". This work is remarkable for its originality and its thinking on international law and international ethics.

Colbert

1619–83, French statesman, who improved the administration of justice, codified the ordinances and reformed the French legal system.

Pothier

1699–1772, French jurist. A scholar of Roman and French law, his monographs on the laws of his country were in many instances incorporated in the French Civil Code. His work on Roman law revealed profound scholarship.

Blackstone

1723–80, English jurist. His *Commentaries on the Laws of England* constitute a standard textbook on the subject, and his fame is perhaps even greater in the United States than in his native land.

Mason

1725–92, American statesman. He succeeded Washington in the Virginia convention and drafted the Bill of Rights, basic to the Constitution of the United States, as well as the Constitutions of many of the States of the Union. Mason's influence extended to the French Declaration of the Rights of Man.

Napoleon I

1769–1821, Emperor of France. He directed the codification of French law, the *Code Napoleon,* which is the basis for the law of France, and has been adopted in many parts of Europe. Actually the work of the most eminent lawyers of France of that time, it combined old French laws with laws envisaging the new revolutionary legal philosophy of France and with the laws conceived by Napoleon himself.

Jefferson

1743–1826, third President of the United States, author of the Declaration of Independence and of the statute of religious freedom in the constitution of Virginia. He is among a small handful of American statesmen who have exerted a major and continuing influence on the basic institutions of the United States, and on the free world, and who is a foremost American immortal in world history.

Architects of the Capitol

Responsibilities of the Architect of the Capitol

George M. White, Architect of the Capitol (third from right) meets with Senator Charles McC. Mathias, Jr., of Maryland, Chairman, Senate Rules and Administration Committee (second from right); Senator Wendell H. Ford of Kentucky, Ranking Democratic Member, Senate Rules and Administration Committee (third from left) and committee staff members Joseph E. diGenova, Staff Director and Chief Counsel (far right); John B. Childers, Deputy Staff Director (far left) and William McWhorter Cochrane, Democratic Staff Director (second from left).

The incumbent Architect of the Capitol, George M. White, FAIA, is the ninth holder of this office, first occupied by Dr. William Thornton, who was appointed by President Washington in 1793 after his design for the permanent Capitol Building in the new Federal capital district was selected winner in a national architectural competition. Dr. Thornton's responsibilities were limited to design and supervision of construction of the new Capitol Building, under direction of the Commissioners of the Federal District and the President of the United States.

The role and responsibilities of the Architect have changed and grown as increased activities have been assigned to the office by the Congress.

The Architect of the Capitol is still charged with the planning, design and construction of such buildings as may be committed to his care by Congress from time to time. Current projects include expansion, modification and enlargement of the facilities of the Capitol Power Plant; construction and equipment of an extension to the Dirksen Office Building; acquisition of additional property as part of the Capitol Grounds; and extension, reconstruction, alteration and improvement of additional House Office Building projects.

The most recent project completed is the construction of the Library of Congress James Madison Builing.

Permanent authority for the care and maintenance of the Capitol Building is provided by the act of August 15, 1876 (19 Stat. 147; 40 U.S.C. 162–163). Appropriate legislation has been enacted from time to time to provide for the care and maintenance of the additional buildings and grounds placed under the jurisdiction of the Architect of the Capitol by Congress over the years.

Although appointment to the office is made by the President, the Architect then becomes a part of the Legislative Branch and serves as an officer and agent of the Congress.

The Architect is charged with the direction and supervision, as well as with the structural and mechanical care, of all improvements, alterations, additions and repairs to the following buildings and grounds, including operation of the mechanical equipment:

Capitol Building (including domestic care of the building except for the Senate Wing)

Capitol Grounds

Senate Office Buildings (including domestic care)

House Office Buildings (including domestic care)

Library of Congress Buildings and Grounds

United States Supreme Court Building and Grounds

Capitol Power Plant

Senate Garage

Robert A. Taft Memorial

The Architect performs his duties in connection with the Senate side of the Capitol, the Senate Office Buildings and the Senate Garage, subject to the approval of the Senate Committee on Rules and Administration as to matters of general policy; in connection with the House Office Buildings and the Capitol Power Plant, his activities are subject to approval and direction of the House Office Building Commission; and he is under the direction of the Speaker in matters concerning the House side of the Capitol.

The Architect is also charged with the operation of the:

United States Botanic Garden (as Acting Director, under the direction of the Joint Committee on the Library)

Senate Restaurants (under the direction of the Senate Committee on Rules and Administration)

William Thornton

Early schooling in Lancashire, England. Spent 3 years at University of Edinburgh studying medicine. Was graduated in 1784 with M.D. from Aberdeen University. Co-experimented with John Fitch in designing a steamboat. Self-taught architect and portrait painter. Won the competition for designing the United States Capitol in 1793. As Architect, supervised the beginning construction of the original North or Senate wing. Appointed as one of three District Commissioners, he continued supervising construction of the Capitol. Superintendents during this period were Stephen Hallet, James Hoban and George Hadfield.

William Thornton

Born May 20, 1759, Jost van Dyke, West Indies. Died March 28, 1828, Washington, D.C. Appointed by President George Washington, 1793. Resigned September 12, 1794.

Benjamin Henry Latrobe

Classic education at Fulneck School, Yorkshire, England. Entered college at Niesky and tradition says he also studied 3 years at University of Leipzig. Studied engineering with John Smeaton and entered the office of S. P. Cockerell, architect. Fellow of the American Philosophical Society; member of American Antiquarian Society and Philadelphia Academy of Arts; vice president of Society of Artists of the United States; honorary member of Academy of Arts; member of Chemical Society of Philadelphia. Constructed the original House wing and remodeled the interior of the original Senate wing; after the fire of 1814 he redesigned and constructed the interiors of both wings, now Statuary Hall and the Old Senate Chamber.

Benjamin Henry Latrobe

Born May 1, 1764, England. Died September 3, 1820, New Orleans, Louisiana. Appointed by President Thomas Jefferson, March 6, 1803—resigned July 1, 1811. Appointed by President James Madison April 6, 1815—resigned November 20, 1817.

Charles Bulfinch

Classic education at Latin School, Boston, Massachusetts, was graduated from Harvard in 1781. Studied architecture in Europe and became New England's leading architect. Member of the National Academy of Design. One of the first American born architects of distinction. Constructed the center section and the original low wooden dome of the Capitol. His design also extended the West Front from that planned by Latrobe. He planned the landscaping and the original earthen west terraces.

Charles Bulfinch

Born August 8, 1763, Boston, Mass. Died April 15, 1844, Boston, Mass. Appointed by President James Monroe January 8, 1818. Office abolished June 25, 1829.

1829 to 1851

From 1829 to 1851 there was no Architect of the Capitol because the office had been abolished. Necessary services were performed by the Commission of Public Buildings and Grounds until 1836 when the Architect of Public Buildings, Robert Mills, was put in charge of maintenance. He was never Architect of the Capitol.

57

Thomas Ustick Walter

Apprenticed as a young boy to his father who was a bricklayer and mason. Strong education in mathematical studies, physical sciences, cultivation of the arts of drawing and painting, and practical knowledge of mechanical construction. Student of architecture and mechanical drawing in the office of William Strickland. Became a practicing architect in 1830. Sent to Europe by the Building Committee of Girard College to study building improvements in general. One of the founders of the American Institute of Architects and its second president; member of Franklin Institute of Pennsylvania and American Philosophical Society; honorary M.A. from Madison University in New York, 1849; Ph. D. from University of Lewisburg, Pennsylvania in 1853; and LL.D. from Harvard, 1857. Won the competition for the design to extend the wings of the Capitol and executed this work; was architect for the present high, iron dome; reconstructed interior of west center building to provide for the Library of Congress after the fire of 1851. Made first studies for extending the East and West Central Fronts of the Capitol.

Thomas Ustick Walter
Born September 4, 1804, Philadelphia, Pa. Died October 30, 1887, Philadelphia, Pa. Appointed by President Millard Fillmore June 11, 1851. Resigned May 26, 1865.

Edward Clark

Studied freehand and mechanical drawing under his architect father, James Clark. Received special training in engineering from his uncle, Thomas Clark, an Army engineer. Student of Thomas U. Walter, and under him was made superintendent of construction on the Patent Office and Post Office in 1857 and assistant to Walter in adding the wings and dome to the Capitol. Fellow in American Institute of Architects and well known in many scientific, literary and musical societies. Oversaw completion of the porticoes of the new wings; reconstructed the Old Hall of Representatives for use as Statuary Hall; extended Capitol Grounds and built present granite terraces; reconstructed and repaired Old Supreme Court section after explosion and fire of 1898; replaced gas with electricity; reconstructed West central floors vacated by Library of Congress when it moved to its present building in 1897; supervised installation of elevators, fireproofing, incandescent lights, modernized heating and ventilation.

Edward Clark
Born August 15, 1822, Philadelphia, Pennsylvania. Died January 6, 1902, Washington, D.C. Appointed by President Andrew Johnson August 30, 1865. Died in office January 6, 1902.

Elliott Woods

Educated in Indianapolis, Indiana. Associated with Architect's office 17 years prior to his appointment as Architect. Also served as architect or associate architect in the erection of public buildings in Washington, D.C. Deeply interested in scientific pursuits, he became known for his work in X-ray and radio and telegraphy. Member of American Institute of Architects. Oversaw the erection of the first House and Senate Office Buildings and subways; built the Capitol Power Plant; added 5th floor to Cannon House Office Building; built 28 rooms in the space formerly occupied by the Library of Congress in the Capitol; made significant changes in lighting, heating and ventilation.

Elliott Woods
Born February 2, 1865 near Manchester, England. Died May 22, 1923, Spring Lake, New Jersey. Appointed by President Theodore Roosevelt February 19, 1902. Died in office May 22, 1923.

David Lynn

Educated in public schools of Cumberland, Maryland and the Allegany County Academy. Entered the Office of the Architect under Edward Clark and became 7th Architect of the Capitol 21 years later upon the death of Elliott Woods. Honorary member of American Institute of Architects. Responsible for construction of the Longworth House Office Building; U.S. Supreme Court Building; Library of Congress Annex; First Street wing of the Old Senate Office Building; built the Senate Garage and expanded the Capitol Grounds; added to the power plant; remodeled the Senate and House Chambers; constructed the Botanic Garden Conservatory; and began construction of the New Senate Office Building.

David Lynn

Born November 10, 1873, Wheeling, West Virginia. Died May 25, 1961, Washington, D.C. Appointed by President Calvin Coolidge August 22, 1923. Retired September 30, 1954.

J. George Stewart

Early schooling in Wilmington; engineering degree from University of Delaware; licensed professional engineer, State of Delaware; president of his own general construction firm; Representative in Congress, 1935–37; Clerk of the District of Columbia Committee, U.S. Senate; engineer consultant to Lands Division, Department of Justice, and Corps of Engineers. Honorary member of American Institute of Architects, honorary fellow American Registered Architects. Continued the work of his predecessor in construction of New Senate Office Building and connecting subways; continued improvements and expansion of the power plant; approved plans for Taft Memorial and bell tower; prepared the Prayer Room for Congressional use; extended East Central Front of the Capitol and rehabilitated the Dome; responsible for construction of Rayburn House Office Building, connecting subway and the House underground garages; remodeled Cannon House Office Building and prepared plans for full remodeling of Longworth House Office Building; initiated improved interior and exterior lighting of the Capitol; responsible for preliminary plans for the James Madison Memorial Library of Congress Building and extension of the West Central Front of the Capitol.

J. George Stewart

Born June 2, 1890, Wilmington, Delaware. Died May 24, 1970, Washington, D.C. Appointed by President Dwight D. Eisenhower October 1, 1954. Died in office May 24, 1970.

George Malcolm White

Graduate of Massachusetts Institute of Technology with a B.S. and M.S. in electrical engineering; M.B.A., Harvard; J.D., Case Western Reserve; Registered Architect in Ohio and D.C.; Registered Engineer in Ohio, Mass. and D.C.; member of Bar of Ohio and D.C.; and the U.S. Supreme Court; certified by the National Council of Architectural Registration Boards and National Council of Engineering Examiners. A former electronics design engineer; has practiced as an architect and consulting engineer since 1948 and as a lawyer since 1960; former member of the faculty at Case Western Reserve in physics and architecture; Fellow of American Institute of Architects and former Vice President; member of National Panel of Arbitrators of the American Arbitration Association; member of National Society of Professional Engineers; member of American Bar Association; and Gold Medalist of Architects Society of Ohio. Ex-officio, a member of the D.C. Zoning Commission, the D.C. Capitol Police Board, and a Director of the Pennsylvania Avenue Development Corporation. Acting Director of the U.S. Botanic Garden. Responsible for construction of the James Madison Memorial Library of Congress Building; restoration of Old Supreme Court and Old Senate Chambers in the Capitol; design of the extension to the Dirksen Office Building; expansion program for the Capitol Power Plant; master plan for Capitol Hill; revisions to interior of Supreme Court building.

George Malcolm White

Born November 1, 1920, Cleveland, Ohio. Appointed by President Richard M. Nixon January 27, 1971.

Visitors and Guide Service

The Capitol Guide Service.

This grand staircase is one of two that serve the House of Representatives.

The people who visit the Capitol of the United States come for many reasons and from a multitude of backgrounds. The Nation's citizens visit the Capitol with feelings of ownership, pride and unity; they come to see the place where the President is inaugurated, to see the workings of their government, to meet their representatives, to show their children the National Heritage. And from around the world, millions come each year to see one of the greatest living symbols of freedom and self-government.

Before these visitors, the Capitol spreads a story, depicted alike in paintings, sculpture, architecture and daily business—the struggle of a people to govern themselves, to be and to remain free.

It is vital to our form of Government that the people be able to see and hear the machinery of legislation in motion. In the House and Senate Chambers, visitors watch from galleries while the Members of Congress debate the issues of Government.

The people also speak. Many come to seek counsel with their Representatives or Senators. They may need help, or wish to make known their position on matters of legislation.

Perhaps the most important visitors are the students, the young people of the world who visit the Capitol and see its workings, its spirit and its substance. Many have studied the forms and history of U.S. Government, but without these visits they can have little idea of the vast range of activities behind the final acts of legislation.

It is an "open" Capitol. Visitors roam the halls and grounds of the Capitol Hill complex at their leisure. Tours and signs and guidebooks are offered to increase the value of their visiting time.

Groups of individuals may request admittance to the House and Senate galleries from their Representative or Senator. The Member writes a letter to the proper official, requesting that the group be admitted, with a copy of the letter to the group leader, who shows it to the Doorkeeper.

Individuals may also obtain passes for admission to the House Gallery from a Representative; admission to the Senate Gallery is gained by a pass issued by a Senator. The two passes are not interchangeable, and they do not admit the bearer to special events and to the Joint Session of the Congress. House Gallery passes are good for both sessions of Congress. Senate Gallery passes are good for only one session.

One organization is authorized by Congress to provide tours, at no charge, through the interior of the United States Capitol.

The original Guide Service was established in 1876 as an outgrowth of the Philadelphia Centennial and the resultant increased volume of visitors to the United States Capitol Building. Guides were unsalaried employees appointed by the Congress who derived their income from the 25 cent fee that was charged for the tour. This system remained in effect until January 3, 1971, when Title IV, Part 4 of Public Law 91–510 ". . . established an organization under the Congress of the United States, to be designated the 'Capitol Guide Service' . . .".

One of the stops on the tour is a Brumidi corridor.

This "Head of Lincoln" by Gutzon Borglum.

This view of the small Senate Rotunda shows the Latrobe tobacco leaf capitals and a later nineteenth century chandelier.

A reflecting visitor in the Capitol Rotunda.

The size of the Rotunda paintings and sculpted reliefs reflects the giant scale of this area.

Jurisdiction over the Capitol Guide Service was vested in the Committee on Rules and Administration of the Senate and the Committee on House Administration of the House of Representatives. The Capitol Guide Board, composed of the two Sergeants at Arms and the Architect of the Capitol was created to direct, supervise and control the Capitol Guide Service.

Public tours of the Capitol Building are offered between 9:00 a.m. and 3:45 p.m., seven days a week except for Thanksgiving, Christmas and New Year's Day. Tours begin at least every 15 minutes and during the busy season as frequently as every two minutes. They cover as many points of interest as possible coincident with existing conditions within the Capitol Building. Over 67 percent of the visitors to the Capitol visit during the five months of April through August of each year.

There are many works of art in the Rotunda to interest visitors.

A visitor records his
visit to the Capitol.

A Capitol guide
leads a tour.

The center of the
Rotunda floor was
once open. Closed by
Bulfinch this area is
now the spot where
American heroes lay in
state.

Music at the Capitol

Music Maestro, Please

The Capitol and the House and Senate office buildings resound, especially during the spring and summer months, with all types of music. From the majestic inspiration of the National Symphony, and the stirring marches of the military bands to the tunes of Gershwin and the tones of Roberta Flack, the visitors to the Capitol can enjoy whatever suits their taste.

The American Festival Concerts at the Capitol are sponsored by the United States Congress and the Secretary of Interior. They are performed by the National Symphony and have been conducted by such maestros as Aaron Copland, Mstislav Rostropovich, Erich Leinsdorf, and the late Arthur Fiedler. These performances have delighted hundreds of thousands of music lovers from all over the world.

The Service bands, and choral groups, of the Air Force, Army, Marine Corps and Navy provide summer night entertainment for other thousands in concerts that have become a Capitol tradition.

Perhaps more thrilling to the individual musicians concerned are the hundreds of performances every spring by the high school and college bands from all over the United States who perform on the Capitol steps. In addition the Capitol and its various office buildings are filled throughout the year, but especially during the winter holiday season, with the joyous voices of choral groups.

These appearances are arranged well in advance by the Senators or Representatives through the Architect of the Capitol.

Without this music, the Capitol would be a far more somber place indeed.

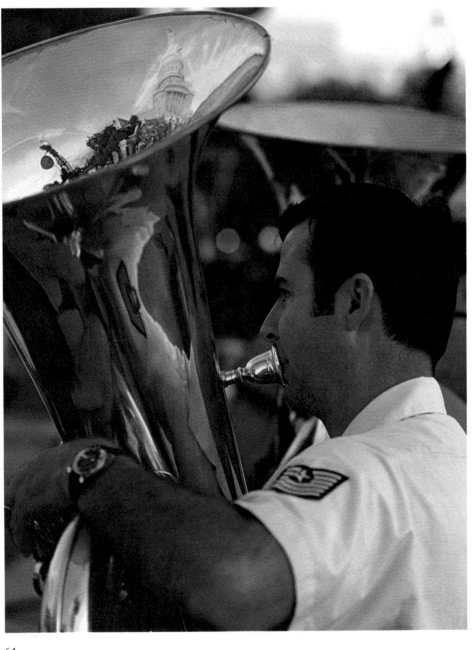

A member of the Air Force Band performs at the Capitol. Note the reflection of the Capitol in the instrument.

The President's Own, the Marine Corps Band performing on the West Front of the Capitol.

The Lake Shore Shorian Marching Band from Michigan on the steps of the West Front of the Capitol.

The National Symphony performs on the West Lawn of the Capitol.

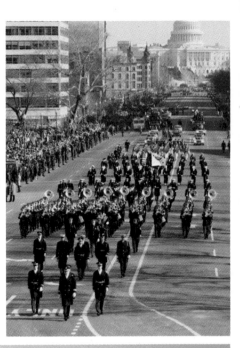

A high school group entertains on the House steps.

The United States Army Band marching down Pennsylvania Avenue from the Capitol.

The Air Force Band performs as hundreds listen on the steps of the West Front of the Capitol.

The Navy Band and Sea Chanters.

The Sea Chanters of the Navy Band performs the Man from La Mancha at the Capitol.

The Marine Corps Band at the Capitol.

A visiting choral group performs in the Russell Senate Office Building Rotunda.

A noontime performance at the Capitol.

A high school band from Sacramento, California, performs at the Capitol.

The Navy Band ceremonial unit.

The Las Estralles del Sol's participating in the American Folklife Series at the Capitol.

Congress as an Institution

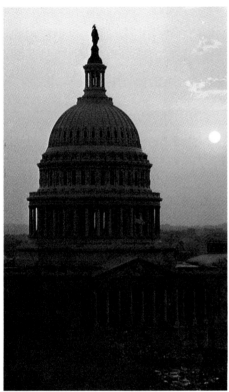

1 Capitol
2 House
3 Senate
4 Russell Senate
  Office Building
5 Dirksen Senate
  Office Building
6 Hart Building (under
  construction)
7 Jefferson Building,
  Library of Congress
  Annex

8 Library of Congress
9 Madison Building,
  Library of Congress
  Annex
10 Cannon House
   Office Building
11 House Annex No. 1
12 Longworth House
   Office Building
13 Rayburn House
   Office Building
14 Botanic Garden

Courtesy of the Architect of the Capitol's Office—1981

The United States House of Representatives

*Official portrait
of the United States
House of Representatives,
April 3, 1981.*

Courtesy of the United States Capitol Historical Society—1981

The Congress was created by Article I of the Constitution which vests all legislative powers granted by the people to the Government in the Senate and the House of Representatives. Section 1 of Article I establishes the specific structure and powers of the House of Representatives.

Currently the House is limited to 435 Representatives elected by the voters of the fifty States. In addition, one Delegate each represents the voters of American Samoa, the District of Columbia, Guam and the Virgin Islands. Puerto Rico is represented by a Resident Commissioner. These latter five persons do not vote on the passage of bills, although they do vote in committee to approve a bill to be considered by the total House.

States are assigned the number of Representatives based on the decennial census. Each Member represents approximately 517,000 constituents. Each State is entitled to at least one Representative, even though the population of the State may be less than 517,000. The State legislature defines the geographic boundaries of the Congressional District whose voters elect a Representative every two years. If a Representative dies or leaves office in mid-term the Governor of the State calls a special election to choose a replacement.

Any citizen over the age of 25, who has been a citizen of the United States for at least seven years, may be elected to serve in the House of Representatives, providing that he or she is a resident of the State at the time of election. Senators must be 30 years of age and a resident of their State.

Unlike the Senate, whose Members represent the States, the Repersentatives' powers do not overlap those of the Executive and Judicial branches of the Federal Government. They do not confirm Presidential appointments. The House does not vote on ratification of treaties. The House can vote on articles of impeachment, i.e., an indictment of the President or other Federal officer, but the Senate judges whether or not the officer is removed from office.

The major strength of the House lies in its power to initiate "money" bills—taxation and appropriation measures. The Senate may vote changes in such bills, but the differences are resolved in conference between the House and Senate.

Because of the large number of Representatives, the House has of necessity developed more restrictive rules on debate than those which apply to the Senate. The Rules Committee of the House determines the order in which bills come to the floor for action, the time limit during which a bill may be considered, whether or not—and how many—amendments to the bill may be proposed.

As in the Senate, the major activity of the House, especially in the early months of each session, is in the committees, which receive all bills introduced on the subject of a committee's jurisdiction. The committees are divided into subcommittees which conduct hearings, add amendments and either approve or reject the bills. If approved, the bill is considered by the full committee which can reject, amend and approve, or decline to act on the measure. If approved, the bill goes to the Rules Committee for scheduling for floor action.

When a bill is granted a rule, it comes before the House which resolves itself into the Committee of the Whole. In this status the House debates the bill, considers and accepts or rejects amendments. The Committee of the Whole then resolves itself into the House of Representatives and votes on each amendment and lastly on final passage.

The House meets in the House Chamber in the South wing of the Capitol. Members are not assigned specific seats as in the Senate, the Majority party members sit on the right of the Speaker's rostrum. The Minority on the left. As in the Senate Chamber, the press and media galleries are above the Speaker's rostrum. The public is seated in the side and rear galleries; seats are available to those who secure passes from their Representatives on a first come, first served basis.

The Mace of the House of Representatives, topped by a flying eagle, is the ensign of authority. Its significance is not merely symbolic since the position of the Mace is a signal to the Members of the activity taking place in the Chamber. An assistant Sergeant at Arms sets it at the right of the Speaker when the House is called to order each day. There it remains in position while the House is in session. Its removal to a lower pedestal means the House has resolved itself into a Committee of the Whole House on the State of the Union. Thus Members can see whether the House is in session or in committee. These signals are important because 218 Members constitute a quorum for action in the House and only 100 when the House is assembled in the Committee of the Whole. William Adams of New York reproduced this 46-inch Mace in 1841 from the design of its predecessor which the British destroyed by fire in 1814. It is a superb example of the silversmith's art, but cost the U.S. only $400. Today it is worth much more and historically and sentimentally it is beyond value.

Benjamin J. Guthrie, Sergeant at Arms of the House, holds the Mace, which is the symbol of legislative power and authority in the House of Representatives.

Chamber of the House of Representatives

The President of the United States is the only person allowed to address the Congress in the Chamber of the House of Representatives in a *joint session.* Any other occasion wherein notables address the Congress is referred to as a *joint meeting.*

The Speaker of the House and the President of the Senate sit on the top dais in this set of three. The President, ministers, kings, diplomats, heads of state and public personalities of the first magnitude, in addressing a joint gathering of Members of the House and Senate in this Chamber, speak from the intermediary dais.

The United States flag is centered behind the Speaker's desk, flanked on either side by the fasces—rods and ax—symbols of the authority of the ancient Roman magistrates, and part of the classical motif which permeates the Capitol. The doors on each side of the dais lead to the Speaker's lobby. Full length portraits of Washington and Lafayette hang to the left and the right of the doors.

Above the clock is the gallery for the press. In the other galleries the heavy television, newsreel and photographic equipment of the communications industry is located. This Chamber has three times the floor area of the British House of Commons and is the largest national parliamentary room in the world. Here for the verdict of Congress were heard the Presidential messages that took the country into war, mobilizing 4,355,000 men in World War I and more than 16,000,000 in World War II.

The flag behind the Speaker, the brass fasces on either side of the flag, the American eagle surrounded by 50 stars in the center of the ceiling, and the colorful seals of each State forming the border decoration of the ceiling are symbols of our freedom in this historic Chamber that the House has occupied since 1857.

In 1973, an electronic voting system was installed to expedite the voting process. Components of this system are located on the walls behind and above the Speaker.

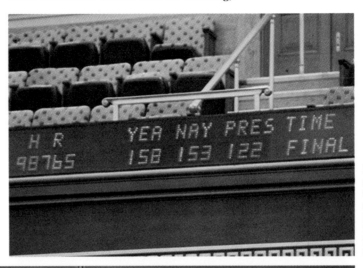

Located below the galleries on each side of the House Chamber, summary display panels present running tabulations as well as the time remaining for the vote in progress.

An individual Representative's vote is displayed on panels above the Speaker's chair while a vote is in progress in the House Chamber.

The Speaker

Foremost Man of His Party in the House. The Speaker of the House is Third in Line and Second in Succession to the Presidency.

It would do no violence to the truth to call the Speaker of the House the second most powerful office holder in the U.S. Government, surpassed only by the President. In fact, the Presidential Succession Act of 1947 places the Speaker second in line in succession to the Presidency, behind only the Vice-President, whose assumption to that office is required by the Constitution.

Selecting a Speaker

In the early days the Speaker was elected by ballot, but since 1839 all have been chosen by roll call or voice vote. The election of the Speaker is traditionally the first order of business upon the convening of a new Congress.

The choosing of the Speaker has undergone a few significant changes over the past 190 years. Only relatively senior members with 20-plus years of experience have been elected Speaker in this century. From 1789 to 1896,

each new Speaker averaged only seven years of experience in Congress. Once elected, a Speaker is customarily re-elected as long as his party remains in the majority and he retains his Congressional seat.

Although the election officially occurs on the floor of the House, modern-day Speakers are actually decided upon when the majority party meets in caucus on the eve of a new Congress. Despite the forgone conclusion of the contest, the minority party also nominates its candidate who, upon losing, becomes minority leader. Since the 1930s, service in the lesser party leadership posts, such as majority and minority whip, majority and minority leader, have become stepping stones to the Speakership.

The stability of the two party system in the modern era has led to a period of unbroken lines of succession in the leadership tracks of both parties. This has not always been the case, however. In 1855, more than 130 separate votes were required over a period of two months before a Speaker was finally chosen. In 1859, only four years later, the House balloted 44 times before choosing a first-term New Jersey Congressman for the Speakership—and he was defeated for re-election *to the House* after that one term.

Powers and Duties

The Constitution makes but scant reference to the office, prescribing in Article I, Section 2 that "the House of Representatives shall chuse [sic] their speaker". While the powers and duties of the Speaker are spelled out to some degree in the *Rules of the House,* the effectiveness of any particular Speaker has depended upon a great many intangibles: the Speaker's own personal dynamism, the size of his majority in the House, his relationship with the executive branch, his ability to "get things done". Men of greatly differing styles and temperaments have served as Speaker. Freshmen, septuagenarians, dictators, tyrants, moderates, Southerners, Northerners, one future President, two future Vice Presidents (and

The Speaker meets with the President and Vice President in his Capitol office.

74

would-be Presidents) have all, at one time or another, served in the Speaker's Chair.

In the modern era, the many duties of the Speaker include presiding at the sessions of the House, announcing the order of business, putting questions to a vote, reporting the vote and deciding points of order. He appoints the chairmen of the Committee of the Whole and members of select and conference committees. He chooses Speakers pro tempore and refers bills and reports to the appropriate committees and calendars. Although he is not constitutionally required to be an elected Member of the House, this *de facto* requirement assures that the Speaker also enjoys the privileges of ordinary House Members. He may, therefore, after stepping down from the Chair, vote and participate in debate on the floor.

Perhaps the duties of the Speaker were put most idealistically by the first "great" Speaker, Henry Clay, back in 1823. It was up to the Speaker to be prompt and impartial in deciding questions of order, to display "patience, good temper and courtesy" to every Member, and to make "the best arrangement and distribution of the talent of the House", in carrying out the country's business. Finally, Clay noted, the Speaker must "remain cool and unshaken amidst all the storms of debate, carefully guarding the preservation of the permanent laws and rules of the House from being sacrificed to temporary passions, prejudices or interests". But in fact the Speakership today is a partisan office. As Floyd Riddick, Parliamentarian Emeritus of the U.S. Senate, has commented, "tradition and unwritten law require that the Speaker apply the rules of the House consistently, yet in the twilight zone a large area exists where he may exercise great discrimination and where he has many opportunities to apply the rules to his party's advantage".

Triple Personality

The Speaker of the House is a triple personality, being a Member of the House, its presiding officer and leader of the majority party in the Chamber. As a Member of the House he has the right to cast his vote on all questions, unlike the President of the Senate (the Vice President of the United States) who has no vote except in the case of a tie. Usually, however, the Speaker does not exercise his right to vote except to

break a tie or when he desires to make his position known on a measure before the House. As a Member, he also has the right to leave the Chair and participate in debate on the House floor as the elected Representative of his district.

As presiding officer of the House, the Speaker interprets the rules that the House has adopted for guidance. In this matter he is customarily bound by precedents, created by prior decisions of the Chair. Appeals are usually in order from decisions of the Chair, but seldom occur. When they are taken, the Chair is usually sustained. The Speaker's power of recognition is partially limited by House rules and conventions that fix the time for considerations of various classes of bills.

He has discretion in choosing the Members he will recognize to make motions to suspend the rules on days when such motions are in order. The rules of the House may be suspended

by two-thirds vote on the first and third Mondays of the month, the Tuesdays immediately following those days, and the last six days of the session.

As a party leader, the Speaker had certain additional powers prior to 1910: to appoint all standing committees and to name their chairmen; to select members of the Rules Committee; and from 1858 to serve as its chairman. His political power evolved gradually during the nineteenth century and peaked under the leadership of former Speaker Joseph Cannon.

In 1910, the House cut back some of the Speaker's power. They removed him from the Rules Committee, stripped him of his power to appoint the standing House committees and their chairmen and restricted his former right of recognition. These actions were not directed so much against the principle of leadership as against the concentration of power in the hands of a single individual.

Congressional Medal of Honor winner Roy P. Benavidez (third from left), of El Campo, Texas, is welcomed to Capitol Hill by (from left) House Republican Leader Robert H. Michel of Illinois; Speaker Thomas P. O'Neill, Jr., of Massachusetts; and Majority Leader James C. Wright, Jr. of Texas.

Three Speakers gather at the Capitol—Carl Albert of Oklahoma, Thomas P. O'Neill, Jr. of Massachusetts and the late John W. McCormack of Massachusetts.

Biography in Brief of the Speaker Thomas P. O'Neill, Jr.

The Speaker is constantly speaking around the United States. Here he speaks for a colleague in Philadelphia.

Thomas Phillip "Tip" O'Neill, Jr., of Massachusetts' Eighth District was elected 47th Speaker of the U.S. House of Representatives January 4, 1977.

Speaker O'Neill was born in Cambridge, Massachusetts, on December 9, 1912, son of Thomas P. O'Neill, who had been a bricklayer and later City Councilman, and the former Rose Ann Tolan. He was educated at St. John's Parochial School, and Boston College from which he was graduated in 1936. He worked in the insurance business but government and politics were his main occupation.

At 14 he was campaigning for Al Smith for President, and he ran for the Cambridge City Council while still a senior at Boston College. He lost, but a year later was elected to the Massachusetts House of Representatives. During his 16 years in the State House on Beacon Hill, he was chosen the first Democratic Speaker in the history of the Commonwealth of Massachusetts. After four years as State House Speaker, he was elected to Congress to succeed John F. Kennedy, who was mov-

ing to the U.S. Senate. In Washington, he quickly became a protégé of John W. McCormack and after a term on the Merchant Marine and Fisheries Committee, he became the second sophomore Congressman in history to be named to the powerful Rules Committee.

He was appointed Majority Whip in 1971 and was unanimously elected Majority Leader in 1973 and again in 1975. In 1977, he was elected without opposition as Speaker. He is the eighth Speaker from Massachusetts, a record.

Speaker O'Neill is a determined golfer, card player and sports fan. He was nicknamed for James Edward O'Neill, of the old St. Louis Browns baseball team who compiled a .492 batting average in 1887 by tipping off foul balls until he won walks, which use to count as hits. When he is not in the Speaker's Chair presiding, he is usually found on the House floor talking with his colleagues about the problems of the day.

He is married to the former Mildred Anne Miller. They have five children.

Gavel in hand, the Speaker is the presiding officer in the House, the highest legislative position in the land.

Speaker O'Neill relaxes at his favorite recreation—golf. Weekends find him at the public and private links in Washington or Massachusetts.

Walking the beach at his home on Cape Cod, winter or summer, is a real pleasure for the Speaker.

IN GOD WE TRUST

Millie O'Neill has the Speaker's attention at the annual Democratic Dinner in Washington.

Vice President George Bush of Texas (left), the presiding officer of the Senate and Speaker Thomas P. O'Neill, Jr., of Massachusetts, stand before the assembly of government officials who gather for a joint session of Congress.

The Speaker receives many visitors in his office, but there is a special charm to 6-year-old Mary Melissa Jablonski, the March of Dimes poster child.

Three very good friends meet at the Capitol, (left to right) the late Former Speaker John W. McCormack of Massachusetts, the late Vice President Hubert H. Humphrey of Minnesota and Speaker Thomas P. O'Neill, Jr., of Massachusetts.

Former Speakers

*Facts about Former
Speakers of the House*

*The first Speaker of the United States
House of Representatives was Frederick
A. C. Muhlenberg of Pennsylvania
who was elected to that office in April
1789. Since that time, there have been
46 other Speakers, from 20 different
States, including the present Speaker
Thomas P. O'Neill, Jr. of Massachusetts.*

*Of the 47 Speakers, one, James K.
Polk, of Tennessee, later served as Presi-
dent of the United States, and two,
Schuyler Colfax, of Indiana, and John
Nance Garner, of Texas, later served as
Vice Presidents of the United States.*

*Former Speaker Sam Rayburn of
Texas served as Speaker the longest in
history, over 17 years, having served as
Speaker in the 76th Congress through
the 79th Congress, then the 81st and
82nd Congresses, and 84th Congress
through the first session of the 87th
Congress. John W. McCormack of
Massachusetts has the distinction of the
longest continuous service as Speaker—
almost nine consecutive years. Speaker
Thomas Pomeroy of New York has the
distinction of serving the shortest term
as Speaker—one day, March 3, 1869.*

Frederick A. C. Muhlenberg,
Pennsylvania: The first Speaker of the
House of Representatives. He served during
both the First and Third Congresses, April
1, 1789 to March 3, 1791, and December 2,
1793 to March 3, 1795.

Jonathan Trumbull,
Connecticut: Second to occupy the
Speakership of the House. He presided over
Second Congress from October 24, 1791 to
March 2, 1793.

Jonathan Dayton,
New Jersey: Speaker,
Fourth, and first session of Fifth
Congresses, December 7, 1795 to March 3,
1797, and May 15, 1797 to July 10, 1797.

Theodore Sedgwick,
Massachusetts: Speaker, Sixth Congress,
December 2, 1799 to March 3, 1801.

Nathaniel Macon,
North Carolina: Speaker, Seventh, Eighth, and Ninth Congresses, December 7, 1801 to March 3, 1807.

Joseph B. Varnum,
Massachusetts: Speaker for Tenth and Eleventh Congresses, October 26, 1807 to March 3, 1811.

Henry Clay,
Kentucky: Speaker Twelfth and Thirteenth (resigned), Fourteenth, Fifteenth, first session of the Sixteenth, and Eighteenth Congresses, November 4, 1811 to January 19, 1814, December 4, 1815 to October 28, 1820, December 1, 1823 to March 3, 1825.

Langdon Cheves,
South Carolina: Elected Speaker during second session of Thirteenth Congress, January 19, 1814 to March 3, 1815.

John W. Taylor,
New York: Speaker, second session Sixteenth Congress, and Nineteenth Congress, November 15, 1820 to March 3, 1821, and December 5, 1825 to March 3, 1827.

Philip P. Barbour,
Virginia: Speaker, Seventeenth Congress, December 4, 1821 to March 3, 1823.

Andrew Stevenson,
Virginia: Speaker, Twentieth, Twenty-first, Twenty-second, and first session Twenty-third Congresses from December 3, 1827 to June 2, 1834.

John Bell,
Tennessee: Speaker, first session Twenty-third Congress, from June 2, 1834 to March 3, 1835.

James K. Polk,
Tennessee: Speaker, Twenty-fourth and Twenty-fifth Congresses from December 7, 1835 to March 3, 1839. Eleventh President of the United States.

Robert M. T. Hunter,
Virginia: Speaker, Twenty-sixth Congress, December 16, 1839 to March 3, 1841.

John White,
Kentucky: Speaker of the Twenty-seventh Congress, May 31, 1841 to March 3, 1843.

John W. Jones,
Virginia: Speaker, Twenty-eighth Congress, December 4, 1843 to March 3, 1845.

John Wesley Davis,
Indiana: Speaker, Twenty-ninth
Congress, December 1, 1845 to March 3,
1847.

Robert C. Winthrop,
Massachusetts: Speaker, Thirtieth
Congress, December 6, 1847 to March 3,
1849.

Howell Cobb,
Georgia: Speaker, Thirty-first Congress,
December 22, 1849 to March 3, 1851.

Linn Boyd,
Kentucky: Speaker, Thirty-second, Thirty-
third Congresses, December 1, 1851 to
March 3, 1855.

Nathaniel P. Banks,
Massachusetts: Speaker, Thirty-fourth
Congress, February 2, 1856 to March 3,
1857.

James L. Orr,
South Carolina: Speaker, Thirty-fifth
Congress, December 7, 1857 to March 3,
1859.

William Pennington,
New Jersey: Speaker, Thirty-sixth
Congress, February 1, 1860 to March 3,
1861.

Galusha A. Grow,
Pennsylvania: Speaker, Thirty-seventh
Congress, July 4, 1861 to March 3, 1863.

Schuyler Colfax,
Indiana: Speaker, Thirty-eighth through the
Fortieth Congresses, from December 7,
1863 to March 3, 1869. Later served as Vice
President.

Theodore M. Pomeroy,
New York: Speaker last day of Fortieth
Congress, March 3, 1869.

James G. Blaine,
Maine: Speaker of the Forty-first through
the Forty-third Congresses, from March 4,
1869 to March 3, 1875.

Michael C. Kerr,
Indiana: Speaker, Forty-fourth Congress,
first session, December 6, 1875 to
August 19, 1876.

Samuel J. Randall,
Pennsylvania: Speaker, second session of Forty-fourth through the Forty-sixth Congresses, from December 4, 1876 to March 3, 1881.

J. Warren Keifer,
Ohio: Speaker, Forty-seventh Congress, December 5, 1881 to March 3, 1883.

John G. Carlisle,
Kentucky: Speaker, Forty-eighth through the Fiftieth Congresses, December 3, 1883 to March 3, 1889.

Thomas B. Reed,
Maine: Speaker, Fifty-first, Fifty-fourth, Fifty-fifth Congresses, December 2, 1889 to March 2, 1891, and from December 2, 1895 to March 3, 1899.

Charles F. Crisp,
Georgia: Speaker, Fifty-second and Fifty-third Congresses from December 8, 1891 to March 3, 1895.

David B. Henderson,
Iowa: Speaker, Fifty-sixth and Fifty-seventh Congresses, from December 4, 1899 to March 3, 1903.

Joseph G. Cannon,
Illinois: Speaker, Fifty-eighth through
Sixty-first Congresses, from November 9,
1903 to March 3, 1911.

James Beauchamp Clark,
Missouri: Speaker, Sixth-second through
Sixty-fifth Congresses, from April 4, 1911
to March 3, 1919.

Frederick H. Gillett,
Massachusetts: Speaker, Sixty-sixth
through Sixty-eighth Congresses, from
May 19, 1919 to March 3, 1925.

Nicholas Longworth,
Ohio: Speaker, Sixty-ninth through
Seventy-first Congresses, from December 7,
1925 to March 3, 1931.

John Nance Garner,
Texas: Speaker, Seventy-second Congress,
from December 7, 1931 to March 3, 1933.
He later served as Vice President.

Henry T. Rainey,
Illinois: Speaker, Seventy-third Congress,
from March 9, 1933 to June 18, 1934.

Joseph W. Byrns,
Tennessee: Speaker, Seventy-fourth
Congress, from January 3, 1935 to June 4,
1936.

William B. Bankhead,
Alabama: Elected Speaker, during the
Seventh-fourth Congress, served until
death in Seventh-sixth Congress, June 4,
1936 to September 15, 1940.

Sam Rayburn,
Texas: Elected Speaker during the 76th
Congress, served through the 79th
Congress, then the 81st and 82nd
Congresses, and 84th-87th Congresses (died
after first session) from September 16, 1940
to August 2, 1946, January 3, 1949 to July 7,
1952, and January 5, 1955 to November 16,
1961.

Joseph W. Martin, Jr.,
Massachusetts: Speaker, Eightieth Congress
and Eighty-third Congress, from January 3,
1947 to December 31, 1948, and January 3,
1953 to August 20, 1954.

John W. McCormack,
Massachusetts: Speaker, second session,
Eighty-seventh Congress through
Ninety-first Congress, from January 10,
1962 to January 2, 1971.

Carl Albert,
Oklahoma: Speaker, Ninety-second
through Ninety-fourth Congresses, from
January 21, 1971 to January 3, 1977.

The House Majority Leader Jim Wright

Majority Leader Jim Wright often addresses constitutent groups in his home district in Tarrant County, Texas.

Congressman Jim Wright of Texas was elected Majority Leader of the U.S. House of Representatives in 1976 by a margin of only one vote. Since that time, his colleagues have twice re-elected him unanimously to this important leadership position.

How highly Jim Wright is regarded by his fellow Congressmen was reflected in a confidential survey conducted by *U.S. News & World Report*. The magazine asked each Member of the House to identify his or her most respected and most persuasive colleagues.

"Picked as the most respected House Member was Majority Leader Jim Wright of Texas," the magazine reported. "Wright also was chosen overwhelmingly as the House's most persuasive debater."

Wright was born in Fort Worth, Texas, the city he represents in Congress today. Just as he fights the clock in his daily routine of being Fort Worth's Congressman and House Majority Leader at the same time, in his early years Wright fought the calendar just as hard.

He finished public school in 10 years and was well on his way toward wrapping up his college career in only three when Pearl Harbor was attacked and Wright enlisted in the Army Air Corps. He received his flier's wings and officer's commission at age 19.

He flew combat missions in the South Pacific and holds the Distinguished Flying Cross and the Legion of Merit.

After the war, Wright was elected to the Texas Legislature at 23. At 26 he became the youngest mayor in Texas when he was elected mayor of Weatherford, a city west of Fort Worth. He was elected to Congress at 31 and presently is serving his 14th consecutive term.

He has sponsored major legislation in the fields of foreign affairs, economic development, water conservation and energy.

Of Wright, John F. Kennedy once said: "I know of no other city that is better represented in the Congress than Fort Worth." Wright's constitutents must think so, too. Whenever he is challenged in primary or general elections, he wins by wide margins.

From his Majority Leader's office, Jim Wright talks to his colleagues and helps the Speaker steer legislation through the House.

Congressman Wright, and his wife, Betty, get greetings from then-President Jimmy Carter at a White House function.

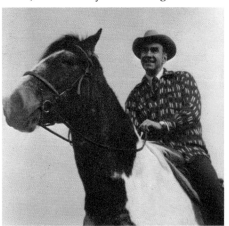

Congressman Wright is proud of the Western heritage of Fort Worth, known as "the city where the West begins."

The House Republican Leader Robert H. Michel

Congressman Bob Michel was elected House Republican Leader of the 97th Congress on December 8, 1980. Prior to that, he served in two other House Republican leadership offices. He was Republican Whip during the 94th, 95th, and 96th Congresses spanning the years 1975–1980. He served as Chairman of the National Republican Campaign Committee during the 93rd Congress from 1973–1974.

Robert Henry Michel was born in Peoria, Illinois on March 2, 1923. He was reared and educated in Peoria and was graduated from Bradley University with a B.S. degree in Business Administration in 1948. Michel received the Bradley University Distinguished Alumni Award in 1961, and an honorary doctorate from Lincoln College in 1977.

During World War II, Michel served in the enlisted ranks as a combat infantryman in England, France, Belgium and Germany. He was wounded by machine gun fire in the Battle of the Bulge and discharged as a disabled veteran after being awarded two Bronze Stars, the Purple Heart and four battle stars.

Michel first came to Washington as the Administrative Assistant to his predecessor, Representative Harold Velde in 1949 and served in that position until 1956. He was elected to the 85th Congress upon Velde's retirement and has been re-elected to 12 consecutive terms since then. He served for a short period on the Committee on Government Operations and in 1958 became a member of the House Appropriations Committee. The Illinois Congressman served on the Appropriations Subcommittee on Agriculture and as ranking Republican on the Labor, Health, Education and Welfare Appropriations Subcommittee and the Legislative Appropriations Subcommittee.

Long active in Republican politics, Michel has been a delegate to every Republican National Convention since 1964 and was chairman of the Platform Subcommittee on Human Resources in 1972 and 1980. Michel was Deputy Floor Leader for President Gerald R. Ford in 1976, and Floor Leader for President Reagan in 1980.

During those rare moments when he is not engaged in Congressional or leadership duties, Congressman Michel is usually found enjoying his two favorite pastimes: singing, in a rich bass voice that has become familiar at gatherings on Capitol Hill, and playing golf. For many years he was the pitcher for the Republican baseball team in its annual duel with Congressional Democrats, winning fifteen out of seventeen starting assignments.

Bob Michel is married to the former Corinne Woodruff of Peoria. The couple has four children, three married sons, Scott, Bruce, and Robin, and a daughter, Laurie.

House Republican Leader Bob Michel of Illinois In His Capitol Office

House Republican Leader Michel flanked by two other newly elected Republican leaders, Congressmen Kemp and Lott.

An accomplished singer, Congressman Michel opened the Republican National Convention in 1980 by singing the National Anthem.

Congressman Michel has participated in a number of golf tournaments for charity over the years.

House Leadership

In his formal office in the Capital (H–204), Speaker Thomas P. O'Neill, of Massachusetts, goes over the day's schedule with his top staff assistants, Gary G. Hymel (left), Eleanor M. Kelley and Leo E. Diehl.

At the beginning of each Congress, the Leadership of the House of Representatives is elected. The Constitution authorizes the House to elect a Speaker. Each party caucus also elects its party leader. Under the tradition of the two party system in this country, the leader of the party with the largest number of Members becomes the Majority Leader. The Minority Leader is invariably the Member nominated by the minority party for the Speaker.

The Majority Leader works very closely with the Speaker in developing the party's position on major policy issues. He almost always has represented a different geographic area of the country from the Speaker. He consults with committee chairmen and urges them to move legislation which the party considers important.

Each party also appoints a whip and assistant whips to assist the floor leader in execution of the party's legislative

The Democratic Leadership of the House of Representatives for the 97th Congress: (left to right) Chief Deputy Majority Whip William V. Alexander, of Arkansas; Majority Whip Thomas S. Foley, of Washington; Majority Leader James C. Wright, of Texas; Speaker Thomas P. O'Neill, Jr., of Massachusetts; and Chairman, Democratic Caucus, Gillis W. Long, of Louisiana.

program. The main job of the whips is to canvass party members on a pending issue and give the floor leader an accurate estimate of the support or opposition expected on a bill. The term "whip" refers to the responsibility of these Members to pressure the other Members of their party to the floor for key votes.

In recent years the majority party has revitalized the Caucus of its Members and the Chairman of the Caucus, elected by his party colleagues, has become an important part of the leadership structure.

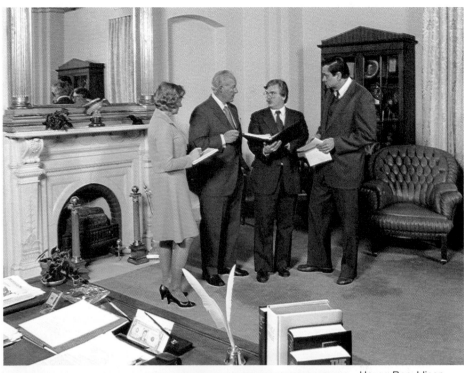

House Republican Leader Robert H. Michel, of Illinois (second from left), in his Capitol Office (H–232) with staff assistants (from left) Sharon G. Yard, William R. Pitts and Hyde H. Murray.

The Republican Leadership of the House of Representatives for the 97th Congress (left to right) Conference Secretary Clair Burgener of California; Policy Committee Chairman Richard Cheney of Wyoming; Minority Whip Trent Lott of Mississippi; Minority Leader Robert H. Michel of Illinois; Conference Chairman Jack Kemp of New York; National Republican Congressional Committee Chairman Guy Vander Jagt of Michigan; Research Committee Chairman Edward Madigan of Illinois and standing behind the Minority Leader is Conference Vice Chairman Jack Edwards of Alabama.

Republican Conference Chairman Jack F. Kemp, of New York (second from left), confers with his Administrative Assistant, David Smick (far left), and Committee staff members Jan Olson and Joe Rogers.

Usually considered as part of the "Leadership" are the chairmen of the twenty-two committees of the House. Until the Congressional reforms in 1975 the Chairmen achieved their status solely by virtue of their seniority. Currently, chairmen are elected by the majority party Caucus, by secret ballot. Committee Chairmen are nominated by the Steering and Policy Committee composed of House leaders, their nominees and Members elected by the Caucus on a regional basis.

House Minority Whip Trent Lott, of Mississippi (left), discusses legislation with his Administrative Assistant, David J. Hoppe, in the Minority Whip's Office (1622 LHOB).

House Majority Leader James C. Wright, of Texas (second from left), in his Capitol Office (H–148) with Administrative Assistant Marshall L. Lynam (seated on left), Executive Assistant Katherine Mitchell and Executive Floor Assistant John Mack (seated on right).

Representative Benjamin S. Rosenthal, of New York, Majority Deputy Whip.

House Majority Whip
Thomas S. Foley, of
Washington (second
from left), in his Capitol
Office (H–107) with
staff assistants (from
left) Lynne P. Brown,
George Kundanis and
Werner W. Brandt.

Deputy Majority Whip
George E. Danielson,
of California (right)
checks the legislative
schedule with his
Administrative
Assistant Raymond W.
Sebens.

Chief Deputy Majority
Whip William V.
Alexander of Arkansas
(second from right)
meets with his top
assistants (left to right)
William J. Miles; Lois
Richardson and Hal
Ponder.

Representative
Geraldine A. Ferraro, of
New York, Secretary,
House Democratic
Caucus.

Representative Gillis
Long, of Louisiana,
Chairman, House
Democratic Caucus.

Elected Officers of the House

At the beginning of each session of Congress both bodies, by majority vote, elect the officers whose responsibility it is to keep the House and Senate operating smoothly. These persons are not Members of the Congress. The House elects the Clerk of the House, the Sergeant at Arms of the House, the Doorkeeper of the House, the Postmaster of the House, and the Chaplain of the House.

Clerk of the House

This office has a broad range of legislative and administrative duties. These include presiding at the opening of each new Congress, pending the election of the Speaker; receiving the credentials of Members; compiling the Official Role of Representatives-elect; taking all votes and certifying passage of bills; processing all legislation, maintaining, printing and distributing documents relating to the legislative activity. The Clerk also receives all official communications during recess or adjournment periods.

A number of internal budgeting, disbursing, accounting and housekeeping responsibilities are also assigned to the Clerk. This officer is assisted by the Offices of Finance, Supply Service, Equipment Service, and Records and Registration. There are 18 various departments that operate under the direction of the Clerk to administer these functions.

Sergeant at Arms of the House

This office enforces the rules of the House and maintains decorum during sessions of the House. The Sergeant at Arms also is in charge of the Mace, the symbol of legislative power and authority.

Maintaining the general security of the House buildings and the Capitol is his major responsibility.

This officer alternates with the Senate Sergeant at Arms as Chairman of the Capitol Police Board and the Capitol Guide Board. Another major responsibility is management of the House bank which disburses Members' salaries and travel expenses.

Benjamin J. Guthrie, Sergeant at Arms.

Edmund Henshaw, Jr., Clerk of the House.

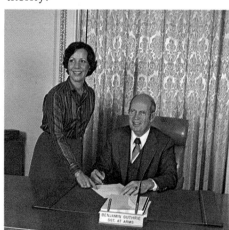

Sergeant at Arms of the House Benjamin J. Guthrie with his Executive Assistant, Pemmie L. Sargent.

Chaplain of the House Reverend James D. Ford with Dianne L. Vogel, Secretary to the Chaplain.

Doorkeeper of the House

Physical arrangements for joint sessions and joint meetings of the Congress, announcements of messages from the President and the Senate, announcement of the arrival of the President when he addresses Congress in person, escorting dignitaries visiting the Capitol—those are the tasks the public sees the Doorkeeper performing. In addition, he supervises the doormen stationed at each entrance to the House floor and House gallery; supervises the pages; operates the Document Room which provides copies of House bills, laws, committee reports, and other documents to the Members, the media and the public on request. Under his jurisdiction are the staff members serving the media galleries and the Members' cloakrooms. He also distributes authorized publications such as the Congressional Directory and copies of the U.S. Codes to the Members and their staffs.

James T. Molloy, Doorkeeper.

Clerk of the House Edmund L. Henshaw, Jr. (center), signs a House Resolution in the presence of Deputy Clerk W. Raymond Colley and Administrative Assistant Ellen Rayner.

Postmaster of the House

The primary duty of the Postmaster is to provide mail pickup and delivery service to the House wing of the Capitol, the House office buildings and the House annexes. Four post offices are under his jurisdiction and provide the usual counter service.

The Postmaster also provides a mail security system which scans every piece of incoming mail. Over 50 million incoming letters and publications are processed annually. Another 50 million or more communications such as the *Congressional Record,* news releases, agency publications also are handled annually.

Chaplain of the House

The Chaplain is responsible for the opening prayer at each session of the House, and occasionally, invites other clergy to serve as guest chaplains. The Chaplain's Office also coordinates use of the Prayer Room and makes arrangements for pastoral services for Members and staff.

Reverend James D. Ford, Chaplain of the House

Robert V. Rota, Postmaster.

James T. Molloy, Doorkeeper, escorts President Reagan and Congressional Leaders to the House floor.

Postmaster of the House Robert V. Rota with staff assistants Nancy Auerbach (left) and Joanna O'Rourke.

The United States Senate

*Official portrait
of the United States Senate,
April 9, 1981.*

The Senate Majority
Leader Howard H.
Baker, Jr. of
Tennessee (left) and
the Senate Democratic
Leader Robert C. Byrd
of West Virginia.

The Senate of the United States is the champion of the States and the co-equal partner of the House of Representatives. On the pediment of the Dirksen Senate Office Building are engraved in marble the words: "THE SENATE IS THE LIVING SYMBOL OF OUR UNION OF STATES."

There are 100 Senators, 2 from each of the States. They are elected for a term of 6 years by a rotating system of elections every 2 years so that "one-third may be chosen every second year". Fifteen times in its history, the Senate has proved to be a training ground for future Presidents of the United States.

The election of Senators by State legislatures, as originally provided in Article I of the Constitution, was abandoned in 1913 with the adoption of the Seventeenth Amendment, providing for direct vote by the people. The election of Senators by direct vote of the people associated the Senate more directly with the people and intensified the truly representative nature of the whole Congress. The Vice President of the United States, says the Constitution, "shall be President of the Senate, but shall have no vote, unless they be equally divided". Whether he wishes to vote or not in the event of such a tie, is a matter of choice with the Vice President himself.

The powers of the Senate overlap into the Judicial and Executive Branches. Thus, the Senate is required to confirm most of the President's appointments. The Senate also ratifies or rejects treaties negotiated by the President with foreign powers. While the House has the power of impeachment, it is the Senate that tries officials who are impeached, and has the aura and authority of a high court.

The Senate and the House enjoy the constitutional power to make their own rules of procedure. In fulfilling its legislative and informing functions, the Senate regulates debate by rules that are more fluid than the rules of the House. Any Senator may speak for as long as he pleases except when debate is limited by the adoption of a cloture motion or by the terms of a unanimous consent agreement.

Bills in the process of becoming law may come to the Senate from the House or go to the House from the Senate. They are thus subject to the advantage of a second look. This doublecheck affords each legislative body a certain appellate function over the other.

A conference of committees of the two Houses generally works out a mutually acceptable compromise on a bill in controversy. Then, passed by both Houses in this final form, it is ready for submission to the President for his signature. Thereupon it becomes law.

This liaison between the two Houses produces deeply considered decisions. It brings to common ground the thinking of the House and the Senate. It develops cooperation.

The end result of this two-way scrutiny of prospective legislation is that it helps to cut to a minimum the margins for error and misjudgment.

Inherent in the bicameral system is the fundamental principle that no State, without its consent, shall be deprived of its equal suffrage in the Senate. Texas or Alaska, New York or California whether dominant in geography, in population, in natural resources or in financial power, cannot in the Senate overwhelm such States, for instance, as Rhode Island or Delaware, Mississippi or Montana, or each other.

Senators Howard H. Baker, Jr. of Tennessee and Robert C. Byrd of West Virginia accept copies of the latest edition of Senate Procedure by the author Senate Parliamentarian Emeritus Floyd Riddick.

Courtesy Alan E. Porter—Senate Photographic Studio

Senate Chamber Desks

When British troops set the Capitol ablaze in 1814, they heavily damaged the Senate Chamber and destroyed its furnishings. As part of the renovation to reopen the Chamber in 1819, the Senate ordered 48 desks at a cost of $34 each from Thomas Constantine, a New York cabinetmaker, who also built the desks for the House of Representatives. Many of these desks remain in the Senate Chamber today, and desks of a similar design have been added as each new State entered the Union.

Over the years several modifications have been made to the desks, primarily to provide more room for the Senators. During much of the 19th century, a Senator's office was his desk on the Senate floor. Beginning in the 1830's three-inch high mahogany writing boxes were added to the desks. Hinged on the top, these writing boxes opened to provide additional space.

Not all Senators preferred the modification, and today one desk still does not have a writing box. This is the Webster desk, which supposedly Daniel Webster refused to have altered on the grounds that if his predecessor could have done without the additional space, so could he. None of Webster's successors have seen fit to abandon that stance. To match its height to the level of others in the Chamber, the desk is raised at its base. Webster had represented Massachusetts in the Senate but had been born in New Hampshire. For many years his desk was occupied by New Hampshire Senators Styles Bridges and Norris Cotton. In 1974, just before Cotton retired from the Senate, he secured adoption of a resolution (S. Res. 467, 93d Cong., 2d sess.) which required that the Webster desk always be assigned to the senior Senator from New Hampshire.

In the mid-nineteenth century mahogany shelves were added at the base of the desks. Later at the turn of the century the legs of the desks were enclosed with a metal grille connected to a plenum chamber below the floor which provided better ventilation. The sanders and inkwells on top of the desks have also undergone change. The original inkwells were made from clear cut glass, covered with square, flat tops that moved horizontally. In 1933, what remained of the original inkwells were replaced by containers with hinged covers because duplicates of the earlier design were no longer being manufactured.

Over the years the desks have been rearranged periodically, as new States sent Senators and as party representation increased and diminished. When additional desks were needed, they were generally contracted out, although the last four desks, for Alaska in 1959 and Hawaii in 1960, were built in the Senate carpentry shop.

The easiest method for tracing the heritage of each desk is to read the names written and carved inside the desk drawers. This appears to be a 20th century tradition, since, for the most part, the earliest recorded names date back only to the first decade of the century. It is possible that 19th century Senators also inscribed their names in the desks, but that these names may have been lost during the refinishing of the drawers.

One difficulty in tracing back the names into the 19th century is that the early Senate Doorkeepers kept such information a closely guarded secret. Isaac Bassett, page and Doorkeeper from 1831 through 1895, feared that relic hunters might destroy the furniture if they knew which pieces were Clay's, Calhoun's and Webster's. Bassett had reasonable cause for alarm, for in 1861 he had stopped the mutilation of one of the Chamber's most famous desks. In April 1861, when the Sixth Massachusetts Regiment was temporarily bivouacked in the Senate Chamber during a recess, Bassett entered the Chamber in time to hear the sound of splitting wood on the Democratic side. Rushing over he found a Union soldier bayonetting the desk vacated by Jefferson Davis, President of the Confederacy. "Stop that; stop that; what are you doing?" Bassett shouted. "That is not Jeff. Davis' desk, it belongs to the Government of the United States. You were sent here to protect Government property, and not to destroy it." Today, a small block of wood inlaid on the left side of the desk (currently occupied by Senator John C. Stennis (D.-Miss.)) covers the spot where the bayonet once struck.

The custom of dividing Senate desks by party is as old as the parties themselves, with Democrats traditionally sitting to the Presiding Officer's right and Republicans to his left. This division, however, has not always been so clear cut.

In the Old Senate Chamber, an equal number of desks were placed on either side of the aisle, without regard to party size. There was no hard rule as to placement, and during the 1840's and 1850's, some Democrats could be found sitting at random on the Whig side. When the Senate moved to its current Chamber in 1859, the practice of dividing the desks equally continued for several years.

The new Chamber was large enough to permit a more flexible seating arrangement, and, in 1877, the practice developed of moving desks back and forth across the center aisle to permit all Members of the majority party to sit together on the appropriate side. From time to time since then, however, one party has elected such an overwhelming majority that it has again become necessary to have majority Members sitting on the minority side. For instance, during the 60th Congress (1907–1909) ten Republicans sat on the Democratic side, while during the 75th Congress (1937–1939) 13 Democrats sat on the Republican side.

Such seating became known as the "Cherokee Strip," meaning that the overflow of majority party Senators were off their reservation. (The Cherokee Strip in Oklahoma referred to land belonging to neither the Indian Territory nor the States.)

The seating of the Majority and Minority leaders at the front row desks on either side of the center aisle is a relatively recent Senate tradition, dating back to 1927 for the Democrats and 1937 for the Republicans.

Daniel Webster's desk.

The Senate Majority Leader

The Majority Leader of the Senate is the closest counterpart of the Speaker of the House, although the Framers of the Constitution apparently did not foresee such a development.

The Constitution's only references to leadership posts in the Senate are contained in two passages of Article I, Section 3. One passage provides that the Vice President "shall be President of the Senate, but shall have no vote, unless they be equally divided" (Clause 4). The other passage provides that the "Senate shall choose . . . a President Pro Tempore, in the absence of the Vice President, or when he shall exercise the office of the President of the United States" (Clause 5). With few exceptions, the Senate has been reluctant to place substantial political power in these offices. It has instead entrusted power to the majority and minority leaders.

Historical studies attempting to explain the Senate's attitude toward these top offices have stressed the unwillingness of Senators to delegate power either to a non-member (the Vice President), or to a Member (the President Pro Tempore) who may preside only at times of the Vice President's absence. If the Vice President and President Pro Tempore are of different political parties, which has often been the case, the Vice President is able to neutralize the authority of the President Pro Tempore by merely assuming the chair. Consequently the Senate has vested the real leadership in its party floor leaders.

Selection

Emergence of readily recognizable floor leaders in the Senate did not occur until 1911–13. Designation of these positions was the culmination of an increasing party influence in the chamber which began around 1890. Before that time leadership in the Senate was usually vested in powerful individuals or small factions of Senators.

In the early years of the twentieth century each party elected its own chairman for the party caucus, but no Senator was elected to be the Majority or Minority Leader as we know these offices today. The "caucus" was in charge of putting through the legislative program.

The Majority and Minority Leaders today are elected by a majority vote of all the Senators in their respective parties. The practice has been to choose the leaders for a two-year term at the beginning of each Congress. After the parties have held their elections, the selection is made known through the press or by announcement to the Senate.

President Reagan and Senate Majority Leader Howard Baker, Jr. of Tennessee discuss legislation at the White House.

Powers and Duties

The Majority Leader is the elected spokesman on the Senate floor for the majority party. The office is a political one, and was not created by the rules of the Senate even though the rules do confer certain powers on the Majority Leader.

The Legislative Reorganization Acts of 1946 and 1970, and more recent amendments to the Senate rules, have given certain unique authorities to the Majority Leader.

The Majority Leader is responsible for the enactment of his party's legislative program. His role is an integral part of the effective functioning of the machinery of the Senate. The Majority Leader must keep himself informed on national and international problems in addition to pending legislative matters. On the floor of the Senate he is charged by his party members to deal with all procedural questions in consultation with them and his party's policy-making bodies. In turn, he must keep his party colleagues informed as to proposed action on pending measures. In more recent years the Majority Leader also has been responsible for the scheduling of legislation.

The Majority Leader acts as a clearinghouse for his party as to the status of pending legislation. He works with party members to secure cooperation and unity in carrying out the party's program. The leader or his designee remains on the floor at all times while the Senate is in session to see that the program is carried out to the party's satisfaction.

The Majority leader almost invariably: (a) offers motions to recess or adjourn from day to day; (b) calls up the *sine die* adjournment resolution and other resolutions relating to adjournment, including resolutions and motions to adjourn for periods of several days; (c) makes motions to proceed to the consideration of all proposed legislation (bills and resolutions); and (d) proffers routine requests to accommodate the Senate, including orders to permit standing committees to meet while the Senate is in session, notwithstanding the provisions of the rule. These are the parliamentary means which enable the Senate to conduct its day-to-day business.

Through the years, the Majority Leader has made the motions to recess or adjourn from day to day, until it is now assumed to be virtually his prerogative.

The Majority Leader keeps in close touch with the Minority Leader as to proposed legislation to be brought up, the procedure to be followed, and the legislative contests to be staged.

In earlier years, even in the 20th century, chairmen of committees usually submitted motions to proceed to the consideration of bills reported by their own committees. At the present time, however, nearly all such motions are made by the Majority Leader.

In summary, the Senate floor leader perfoms six basic functions of leadership. He is, or has the potential for being, the principal force in organizing the party, scheduling business for the Senate, promoting attendance on the floor, collecting and distributing information, persuading other Senators to unite on policy questions and providing liaison with the White House.

President's Room, located in S–216 of the Capitol is the place where many bills were signed by Presidents. Pictured behind the table used by President Lincoln and other chief executives of the United States stands Senate Majority Leader and Mrs. Howard Baker, Jr. of Tennessee (left) and Senate Democratic Leader and Mrs. Robert C. Byrd of West Virginia, talking with two well known Washington reporters, Joseph McCaffrey and Betty Beale.

Biography in Brief of the Senate Majority Leader Howard H. Baker, Jr.

Senator Howard H. Baker, Jr., is the first Republican to be elected to the post of United States Senate Majority Leader in more than a quarter century.

Since 1966, when he became the first Republican ever popularly elected to the Senate from Tennessee, Senator Baker has won re-election twice, in 1972 and 1978, by overwhelming margins.

He was elected Senate Minority Leader in 1977 and was re-elected to that office in 1979 by a unanimous vote of Senate Republicans.

As a candidate for the Republican nomination for President of the United States in 1980, Senator Baker won praise from supporters and competitors alike for his constructive, issue-oriented campaign.

Senator Baker first won national recognition in 1973 as vice chairman of the Senate Watergate Committee, and he was keynote speaker at the Republi-

can National Convention in 1976.

Howard Baker was born November 15, 1925 in Huntsville, Tennessee, and attended public elementary school there. He graduated from McCallie Military school in Chattanooga at age 17 and enlisted in the Navy V–12 program. He studied electrical engineering at the University of the South in Sewanee, Tennessee, and Tulane University in New Orleans. He was commissioned after WW II and served in the Pacific until 1946. He graduated from the University of Tennessee law school in 1949, and joined the law firm founded by his grandfather in 1885. In 1951 Howard Baker and Joy Dirksen, daughter of the late Senator Everett Dirksen, were married. They have two children, Derek, and Cynthia.

Howard H. Baker, Jr.'s association with politics has been life-long. His father, Howard H. Baker, served in the U.S. House of Representatives from

The Majority Leader presents his Party's position before a Senate Committee.

An incisive question is posed by Senator Baker as Chairman Ervin ponders the gravity of the Watergate hearings.

Senator Baker (Minority Leader, 1977 to 1981; Majority Leader, 1981–) is sworn in January 1966, by Vice President Hubert H. Humphrey, with the approval of Majority Leader Mike Mansfield (1961 to 1977) and the late Senator Dirksen (Minority Leader 1959 to 1969).

Photographer Howard H. Baker, Jr. pursues his hobby at the Republican National Convention.

1951 until his death in 1964. His step-mother (his mother died when he was eight) Iris Baily Baker, completed the term. His grandmother, who lived in the Huntsville area, was once a sheriff, died this year at the age of 101. She once advised Senator Baker against seeking the Presidency in 1980 on the grounds that, "If you really want to get close to power, you ought to run for sheriff."

The Majority Leader is an accomplished photographer, whose work has been widely exhibited and acclaimed. His photos appear on several pages of this publication.

Senator Baker once set out his own philosophy of public service in these words: "To overcome the divisions that set people apart, to seek in the midst of discord some common ground where people may stand together, to blend representation with reason, to temper conviction with conciliation, and not only to serve but to lead."

The Majority Leader makes a point to a most distinguished group.

The Majority Leader during one of his frequent TV interviews.

The Bakers—Derek, Joy, Howard and Cynthia—whistle-stopping during his campaign.

Howard H. Baker, Jr., age 5, indicates an early preference for Navy service.

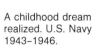

A childhood dream realized. U.S. Navy 1943–1946.

Senator Baker keeps in touch with the voters in Tennessee.

Cynthia Baker and her father unveil the U.S. Postal Service stamp honoring her grandfather, Everett McKinley Dirksen.

101

Former Senate Majority Leaders

Sixteen men have formerly served as Majority Leader of the United States Senate since the emergence of the position in the 62nd Congress. Of the 16 Majority Leaders, the late Alben W. Barkley, of Kentucky and Charles Curtis, of Kansas, later served as Vice Presidents, and the late Lyndon B. Johnson, of Texas, served as Vice President and President. Senator Mike Mansfield, of Montana, has the distinction of having the longest continuous service as Majority Leader, having served from January 3, 1961 until January 3, 1977, for a total of 16 years. Senator Mansfield is now serving as United States Ambassador to Japan.

Shelby M. Cullom
of Illinois: Majority Leader, 62nd Congress, April 4, 1911 to March 3, 1913.

John W. Kern
of Indiana: Majority Leader, 63rd and 64th Congresses, March 5, 1913 to March 3, 1917.

Thomas S. Martin
of Virginia: Majority Leader, 65th Congress, March 6, 1917 to March 3, 1919.

Henry Cabot Lodge
of Massachusetts: Majority Leader, 66th Congress through first session of 68th Congress, from March 4, 1919 to November 9, 1924.

Charles Curtis
of Kansas: the first to actually be called a "floor leader." Majority Leader, first session of the 68th Congress through the 70th Congress, from November 28, 1924 to March 3, 1929. Later served as Vice President of the U.S.

James E. Watson
of Indiana: Majority Leader, 71st and 72nd Congresses, from March 5, 1929 to March 3, 1933.

Joseph T. Robinson
of Arkansas: Majority Leader, 73rd Congress through the first session of the 75th Congress, from March 4, 1933 to July 14, 1937.

Alben W. Barkley
of Kentucky: Majority Leader, 75th Congress, first session, through 79th Congress, July 22, 1937 to January 3, 1947. He is a former Vice President of the U.S.

Wallace H. White, Jr.
of Maine: Majority Leader, 80th Congress, January 3, 1947 to January 3, 1949.

Scott W. Lucas
of Illinois: Majority Leader in the 81st Congress, January 20, 1949 to January 3, 1951.

Ernest W. McFarland
of Arizona: Majority Leader, 82nd Congress, February 22, 1951 to January 3, 1953.

Robert A. Taft
of Ohio: Majority Leader in the 83rd Congress, first session, from January 3, 1953 to July 31, 1953.

William F. Knowland
of California: Majority Leader in the 83rd Congress, from August 4, 1953 to January 3, 1955.

Lyndon B. Johnson
of Texas. This former U.S. President and Vice President served as Majority Leader from the 84th through the 86th Congresses, from January 3, 1955 to January 3, 1961.

Mike Mansfield
of Montana: Majority Leader from the 87th through the 94th Congresses, January 3, 1961 to January 3, 1977.

Robert C. Byrd
of West Virginia: Majority Leader from the 95th Congress through the 96th Congress, January 3, 1977 to January 3, 1981.

The Senate Democratic Leader

A pensive Senate Democratic Leader ponders the problems of the Nation—and the world.

Senator Robert Carlyle Byrd of West Virginia was elected United States Senate Democratic Leader by his Democratic colleagues on January 4, 1977 and reelected unanimously in 1979 and in 1981

This powerful position was achieved by a man of remarkable initiative who has held more legislative elective offices than any other individual in the history of West Virginia.

Born Cornelius Calvin Sale, Jr., on November 20, 1917, in North Wilkesboro, North Carolina, he was sent to live with his aunt and uncle, Vlurma and Titus Byrd, of Stotesbury, West Virginia, after his mother died in the influenza epidemic of 1918. He thus acquired the name Robert Byrd from his adoptive parents.

Educated in West Virginia public schools, he graduated valedictorian of the 1934 class of Stotesbury's Mark Twain High School. Because of the depression, he could not afford to go to college. Later, however, he earned his law degree, graduating *cum laude* from American University in Washington, D.C., an accomplishment achieved by

attending night school for 10 years while serving in the United States House of Representatives and Senate.

Senator Byrd, who was employed in a grocery store in southern West Virginia when he initially became interested in politics, was first elected to the West Virginia House of Delegates and later to the West Virginia Senate. He was elected to the United States House of Representatives in 1952, serving three terms before being elected to the United States Senate in 1958.

In the Senate, Senator Byrd sought and obtained a seat on the influential Appropriations Committee, and today also serves on the Judiciary and Rules and Administration Committees. In January 1967, Senator Byrd was elected Secretary of the Senate Democratic Conference and in 1971 was chosen Senate Democratic Whip, a position he held until being elected Democratic Leader.

The Democratic Leader is an accomplished musician who is dedicated to preserving the Bluegrass and Appalachian mountain music that is so much a part of West Virginia's heritage. He plays the violin as a hobby, and has performed his music on various national television programs.

Senator Byrd is married to the former Erma Ora James. They have two daughters and six grandchildren.

President Reagan welcomes the Senate Democratic Leader to the White House.

A young Robert C. Byrd (right) helps carry lunch pails to the local boarding house in West Virginia.

The Senate Democratic Leader meets the Press.

The Senate
Democratic Leader
"does his homework".

Senator Byrd spends a
few moments with two
friends.

Vice Chairman Deng Xiao
Ping of the People's
Republic of China and
the Senate Democratic
Leader.

Senator Russell Long
of Louisiana confers
with the Senate
Democratic Leader on
tax legislation.

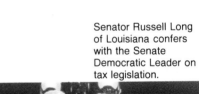

Senator Byrd attends a
reception at the
Botanic Garden.

Senator and Mrs. Byrd
keep close contact with
West Virginia voters,
rain or shine.

Senator Byrd plays the
fiddle at a Democratic
Dinner.

Graduate of American
University law school.

105

Senate Leadership

Senate Majority Leader Howard H. Baker, Jr. of Tennessee in his Capitol office (S-230) with his Executive Secretary, Lura Nell Triplett; Howard S. Liebengood, Senate Sergeant at Arms, and William F. Hildenbrand, Secretary of the Senate.

Republican Leadership for the 97th Congress (left to right); Senators Bob Packwood of Oregon, Chairman, National Republican Senatorial Committee; Ted Stevens of Alaska, Majority Whip; Howard H. Baker, Jr. of Tennessee, Majority Leader; James A. McClure of Idaho, Chairman, Republican Conference; Edwin (Jake) Garn of Utah, Secretary, Republican Conference; John Tower of Texas, Chairman, Republican Policy Committee and Strom Thurmond of South Carolina, President Pro Tempore of the Senate. This photograph was taken by the Senate Photographic Studio in the original Senate Chamber located in Room S-228 of the Capitol.

The Constitution requires that the Vice President is the President of the Senate. Since the Vice President is frequently not present in the Senate, except in the case of a close vote which may end in a tie, the Senate elects a President pro tempore; by custom, in recent decades, the most senior majority party Member of the Senate. The President pro tempore is a key member of his party's policymaking body. He usually designates a more junior Senator to preside over daily sessions in his place. The President pro tempore also has the responsibility for the Legislative Counsel, a group of legal specialists who assist Senators in drafting bills.

Since the early days of the twentieth century, the Senate has, by custom developed the position of Majority Leader as a parallel in power to the Speaker of the House.

The real leader of the Senate is the Majority Leader. He is the legislative strategist and exercises considerable influence on committee assignments.

The Majority Leader is elected by the Senators who are members of the political party to which more than 50 percent of the Senators belong. The Senators of the party with the lesser number elect a Minority Leader.

In cooperation with their party organization, each Leader is responsible for the achievement of the legislative program. They manage the order in which legislation moves to passage and expedite noncontroversial legislation. They keep members of their party informed regarding pending business. Each Leader is an ex-officio Member of his party's policymaking and organizing body. Each is aided by an assistant Leader, called the Whip, as in the House, and by the Majority or Minority Secretary, who are professional staff administrators, but not Members of the Senate.

Each of the two major parties in the Senate is organized differently. The Democrats have a caucus which nominates the Leader , elects the Steering Committee and approves Steering Committee nominations for Committee Chairmen. The Steering Committee nominates Committee Chairmen and assigns party members to Committees. The Democratic Policy Committee develops legislative policy and positions.

The Republican Senators comprise the Republican Conference which elects the Republican Leader and deals with procedural matters. The Conference Committee assigns party members to Committees. They also elect the Republican Policy Committee which handles the research and policy determination function of the party.

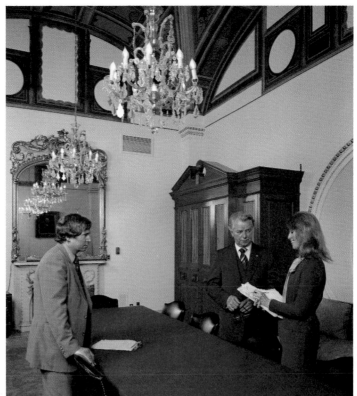

Senate Democratic Leader Robert C. Byrd of West Virginia discusses the legislative schedule with his Executive Secretary, Barbara Videnieks and Press Secretary, J. Michael Willard. The Democratic Leader's office is located in Room S–208 of the Capitol.

The Senate Democratic Leadership for the 97th Congress (left to right); Senators Wendell H. Ford of Kentucky, Chairman, Democratic Senatorial Campaign Committee; Daniel K. Inouye of Hawaii, Secretary of the Democratic Conference; Robert C. Byrd of West Virginia, Senate Democratic Leader and Alan Cranston of California, Senate Democratic Whip. This photograph was taken by Alan E. Porter of the Senate Photographic Studio in the President's Room located in Room S–216 of the Capitol.

Senate Minority Whip Alan D. Cranston of California, left, in his Capitol office (S–148) with Administrative Assistant Roy F. Greenaway.

Senator Edwin (Jake) Garn of Utah, Secretary Senate Republican Conference.

Senator Daniel K. Inouye of Hawaii, Secretary, Senate Democratic Conference.

Senator Strom Thurmond of South Carolina, President Pro Tempore of the Senate.

Senator John G. Tower of Texas, Chairman, Republican Policy Committee.

Senator Wendell H. Ford of Kentucky, Chairman, Democratic Senatorial Campaign Committee.

Senator Ted Stevens of Alaska, Majority Whip of the Senate.

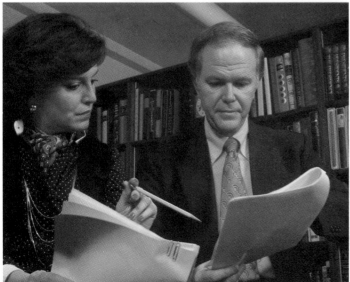

Senate James McClure of Idaho, Chairman, Republican Conference Committee.

National Republican Senatorial Committee Chairman Bob Packwood of Oregon reviews floor statement with his Administrative Assistant Mimi Weyforth.

Elected Officers of the Senate

At the beginning of each session the Senate elects its officers for a two year term. These oficers are: the Secretary of the Senate, the Sergeant at Arms of the Senate, the Majority and Minority Secretaries of the Senate and the Chaplain of the Senate.

Secretary of the Senate

The primary duty of this officer is for the legislative administration of the Senate. He is custodian of the Senate Seal; administers oaths of office; certifies passage of legislation; ratification of treaties and confirmation or rejection of Presidential nominations. He is assisted in his legislative administration by a wide variety of experts, including the Parliamentarian, Legislative Clerk, Office of Classified National Security Information, Journal Clerk, Disbursing Officer, Senate Librarian, Senate Historian and official reporters, among others. He also is a member of the Federal Election Commission, the Federal Council on the Arts and Humanities and serves as Executive Secretary to the Commission on Art and Antiquities of the Senate.

William F. Hildenbrand
Secretary of the Senate

Sergeant at Arms of the Senate

The responsibility of the Sergeant at Arms of the Senate is primarily to enforce the rules of the Senate and maintain decorum. In addition, he supervises the computer and micrographic centers, Senate post offices, press galleries, service department, recording studio, telephone services and janitorial services. He rotates with the House Sergeant at Arms as chairman of the Capitol Police Board and the Capitol Guide Board. He also is the protocol officer of the Senate, including the announcement of the arrival of the President and other dignitaries.

Howard Libengood
Sergeant at Arms

Secretary to the Majority, Howard O. Green, Jr. (right) and Assistant Secretary to the Majority John C. Tuck compare their notes on the days floor activities.

Reverend Halverson, Chaplain of the Senate, checks his calandar with his assistant, Allie Johnson.

Secretaries to the Majority and the Minority

The Secretary to the Majority and the Secretary to the Minority are also elected officers of the Senate. Their duties are similar—primarily to supervise the majority and minority cloakrooms, obtain pair votes for Senators as requested, brief Senators on votes and issues under consideration, poll the Senators at the request of the Leadership and in general serving the Senators who comprise the majority and minority.

Howard O. Greene, Jr.
Secretary to the
Majority

Walter J. (Joe) Stewart
Secretary to the
Minority

Chaplain of the Senate

The Chaplain of the Senate serves as pastor, to the Senators and their families. He opens the sessions of the Senate each day with prayer. His office is a resource center for information concerning the Bible, various denominations and the subject of religion in general.

Reverend
Richard C. Halverson
Chaplain of the Senate

Senate Sergeant at Arms, Howard S. Libengood (left) checks the days schedule with his deputy, Larry E. Smith.

Secretary of the Senate, William F. Hildenbrand discusses matters of the Senate with his Deputy, Marilyn Courtot.

Secretary to the Minority, Walter J. (Joe) Stewart reviews the Senate legislative schedule with his Administrative Assistant Jeanine Drysdale Lowe.

Five Outstanding Senators

Adjacent to the Senate Chamber on the second floor of the Senate wing of the Capitol is the Senate Reception Room.

Aside from "real live Senators" who leave the Senate floor to confer with constituents, government officials, lobbyists and visitors during sessions of the Senate, the most impressive feature of the Senate Reception Room is the series of portraits of five former U.S. Senators selected as outstanding among all the persons who served in the U.S. Senate before 1959, the year the por-

traits were placed in the five hitherto empty spaces.

A Special Senate Committee on the Senate Reception Room was established by a resolution of the 84th Congress. Senator John F. Kennedy (D–Massachusetts) was named Chairman. The other members of the Committee were: Senators Richard B. Russell (D–Georgia), Mike Mansfield (D–Montana), John W. Bricker (R–Ohio) and Styles Bridges (R–New Hampshire). The committee was

From left to right; Senate Majority Whip Ted Stevens of Alaska; Democratic Whip Alan Cranston of California; Democratic Leader Robert C. Byrd of West Virginia and Majority Leader Howard H. Baker, Jr., of Tennessee meet prior to Senate going into session in the Senate Reception Room (S–213) just off the Senate floor.

charged with the duty of selecting "five outstanding persons from among all persons, but not a living person, who have served as Members of the Senate since the formation of the Government of the United States whose painting shall be placed in the five unfilled spaces in the Senate reception room".

The Chairman of the Special Committee, Senator John F. Kennedy, was the chief organizer and proponent of the project to select the outstanding senators. During long months of convalescence from back surgery to correct damage from injuries received in WWII, Senator Kennedy studied extensively the lives and contributions of great Americans who in times of decision placed the national good above popular opinion. His book, *Profiles in Courage,* was the forerunner of his work on the Special Committee. The Senate resolution also authorized the Committee to consult with "historians and other sources, including the general public as it deems advisable".

The criteria recommended by the advisory committee provided that the five Senators should be chosen without regard for their services in other offices, that they should be distinguished for acts of statesmanship transcending party and State lines, and that their leadership in national thought and constitutional interpretation be considered as well as in legislation.

The Committee reported on May 1, 1957. The report stressed that those selected were "not necessarily the five greatest Senators; nor the most blameless or irreproachable ones, nor models of contemporary behavior. Allowances must be made, moreover, of the times, the morals, and the practices of the period in which each served; and political and policy differences should not diminish their claim to the label outstanding."

The artists commissioned by the Senate were Arthur Conrad for Calhoun, Allyn Cox for Clay, Chester La Follette for La Follette, Dean C. Keller for Taft and Adrian Lamb for Webster.

Five outstanding Senators of the past were chosen by a Special Committee, and approved by the entire Senate

Clay

Senator
Henry Clay,
of Kentucky, who
served in the Senate
1806–7, 1810–11, 1831–42, 1849–52.

Webster

Senator
Daniel Webster,
of Massachusetts,
who served in the Senate
1827–41, 1845–50.

Calhoun

Senator
John C. Calhoun,
of South Carolina, who
served in the Senate
1832–43, 1845–50.

La Follette

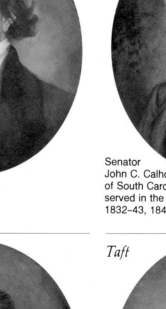

Senator
Robert M.
La Follette, Sr., of Wisconsin,
who served in the Senate 1906–25.

Taft

Senator
Robert A. Taft,
of Ohio, who served in
the Senate 1939–53.

Vice President of the United States and President of the Senate

The Vice President, who is the constitutionally designated presiding officer of the Senate, is a unique figure in our government. He is the only official with duties both in the executive and legislative branches. For many years the Vice President was not much more than "the man in the wings" waiting to fill the void should a vacancy occur in the presidency.

Since Harry Truman's presidency, however, the role of the Vice President has been steadily expanded and now even more than ever, the Vice President does indeed play a key role in our system of Government.

The Constitution states the role of the President of the Senate as follows: "The Vice President of the United States shall be President of the Senate, but shall have no vote, unless they be equally divided." And again the Constitution stipulates: "The Senate shall chuse [sic] their other Officers, and also a President pro tempore, in the Absence of the Vice President, or when

Supreme Court Justice Potter Stewart administers the Oath of Office to the 43rd Vice President of the United States, George Herbert Walker Bush, as Mrs. Barbara Bush holds the Bible and Senator Mark O. Hatfield of Oregon looks on.

The Vice President and Senator Thurmond, President Pro Tempore of the Senate, chat with Mrs. Bush, who is in uniform as a participant in the traditional Senate Wives Red Cross production program.

The Vice President visits House Judiciary Committee Chairman, Peter W. Rodino, Jr. of New Jersey.

The President and Vice President pay a visit to the Capitol.

he shall exercise the Office of President of the United States.''

George Herbert Walker Bush, of Texas, the 43rd man to serve as Vice President, is no stranger to the Capitol, having served in the United States House of Representatives for two terms. His father, the late Prescott Bush, served as United States Senator from Connecticut. The United States Senate confirmed the appointments of the younger Bush as United States Ambassador to the United Nations in 1971 and as Director of the Central Intelligence Agency in 1976. He also served as Chief of the United States Liaison Office in the People's Republic of China in 1974–75.

He served from August 1942 to September 1945 as a Naval aviation cadet and carrier pilot, and fought in the Pacific, winning three Air Medals and the Distinguished Flying Cross.

He is married to the former Barbara Pierce, of Rye, New York. They are the parents of five children and have two grandchildren.

The Vice President and President pose for an official portrait with H. E. Takeo Fukuda, former Prime Minister of Japan.

The President confers with his working Vice President. As did his predecessor, President Carter, President Reagan has made the Vice President a key leader in his administration.

The President and Vice President visit informally at the White House with Great Britain's Prime Minister Margaret Thatcher.

Speaker O'Neill, and Vice President Bush enjoy a joke as they prepare to preside over a 1981 Joint Session of Congress.

The Vice President presides at a Cabinet meeting in the White House. L. to R. Treasury Secretary Regan, the Vice President, Attorney General Smith and Labor Secretary Donavan

The Vice President confers with Senate Majority Leader Howard H. Baker, Jr.

Vice President Bush. Photograph by Senator Howard H. Baker of Tennessee.

Former Vice Presidents of the United States

Forty-two men have formerly served as Vice President of the United States. Of this total, nine were former Members of the House only, eight were former Senators only, and twelve served in both the House and Senate. Three were members of the Continental Congress and one was a member of the Continental Congress and later of the House of Representatives. Ten former Vice Presidents had no previous experience in the Congress. Thirteen Vice Presidents later became Presidents of the United States.

John Adams,
Massachusetts, first President of the Senate and Vice President (1789); second President of the United States.

Thomas Jefferson,
Virginia, presided over the Senate (1797) as Vice President under John Adams; was elected third President of the United States.

Aaron Burr,
New Jersey, was Jefferson's Vice President (1801), an able but disturbed politician whose duel with Hamilton and sad decline ruined his place in history.

George Clinton,
New York, Vice President (1805) in Jefferson's second term (an uncle of the better known De Witt Clinton), a member of the Continental Congress in 1775–76; served also as Vice President under James Madison.

Elbridge Gerry,
Massachusetts, was Vice President (1813) under James Madison. A signer of the Declaration of Independence, later elected Governor of Massachusetts.

Daniel D. Tompkins,
New York, Vice President (1817) under James Monroe, was Governor of New York and one of the founders of the New York Historical Society; re-elected with Monroe in 1820.

John C. Calhoun,
South Carolina, Vice President (1825) under John Q. Adams. One of the South's great statesmen. Re-elected Vice President 1828 on the Jackson ticket.

Martin Van Buren,
New York, was Vice President in the Jackson administration (1833) when Calhoun resigned on his election to the Senate. Succeeded to Presidency 1837.

Richard M. Johnson,
Kentucky, Van Buren's Vice President (1837), soldier and Senator, voted into Vice Presidency by the Senate, because regular candidates failed of majority of electoral votes.

John Tyler,
Virginia, Harrison's Vice President (1841), Representative and Senator, Governor, succeeded to Presidency on Harrison's death, was subject of the spirited campaign slogan: Tippecanoe and Tyler, too.

George M. Dallas,
Pennsylvania, James K. Polk's Vice President (1845), Van Buren's Minister to Russia; President Pierce's Minister to Great Britain; one-time Mayor of Philadelphia.

Millard Fillmore,
New York, Zachary Taylor's Vice President (1849), succeeding him to the Presidency when Taylor died, fought in the Civil War on Union side, prominent in state and national politics.

William R. King,
North Carolina and Alabama, Franklin Pierce's Vice President (1853), was a Senator from Alabama after having served as Representative from North Carolina. He also served as President pro tempore of the Senate.

John C. Breckinridge,
Kentucky, James Buchanan's Vice President (1857) in the controversial era before Civil War, youngest Vice President up to that time, defeated for Presidency by Lincoln.

Hannibal Hamlin,
Maine, Abraham Lincoln's Vice President (1861); was Speaker of the State House of Representatives; Senator, Governor of Maine, later Minister to Spain.

Andrew Johnson,
North Carolina and Tennessee, Lincoln's second-term Vice President (1865); totally self-educated; organized and led 1828 working-man's party; Governor of Tennessee and Senator; succeeded Lincoln on latter's death; acquitted of impeachment charges.

Schuyler Colfax,
New York and Indiana, Grant's Vice President (1869); Speaker of House in 38th, 39th and 40th Congresses. Distinguished editor. Completely vindicated of corruption charges in 1873 Credit Mobilier scandal.

Henry Wilson,
New Hampshire and Massachusetts; U. S. Grant's Vice President, succeeding Colfax (1873), owner-editor *Boston Republican,* active in Free Soil politics; Senator; died in Capitol, 1875.

William A. Wheeler,
New York, Rutherford B. Hayes' Vice President (1877); elected Representative to Thirty-Seventh, Forty-First, and three succeeding Congresses, then to Vice Presidency.

Chester A. Arthur,
Vermont and New York, James A. Garfield's Vice President (1881), succeeding to Presidency same year upon Garfield's assassination, held high military posts.

117

Thomas A. Hendricks,
Ohio and Indiana, Grover
Cleveland's Vice President (1885);
Representative and Senator from
Indiana; Governor of Indiana, 1872;
failed Vice Presidential election
with Tilden, 1876.

Levi P. Morton,
Vermont and New York, Benjamin
Harrison's Vice President (1889);
Representative to Forty-sixth and
Forty-seventh Congresses; U.S.
Minister to France 1881–85.

Adlai E. Stevenson,
Kentucky and Illinois, grandfather
of Democratic candidate for
President, 1952 and 1956. He was
Grover Cleveland's Vice President
(1893) and a Member of Congress.

Garret A. Hobart,
New Jersey, William McKinley's
Vice President (1897), held state
elective offices, including
speakership of New Jersey
Assembly. Died 1899 before end of
Vice Presidential term.

Theodore Roosevelt,
New York, William McKinley's
Vice President (1901).
Spanish-American war hero.
Assistant Secretary of Navy;
Governor of New York; President
of the United States.

Charles W. Fairbanks,
Ohio and Indiana, Theodore
Roosevelt's Vice President (1905);
Senator; resigned
Senatorship to run for Vice
President with Roosevelt 1904;
failed to be reelected (with Hughes)
1916.

James S. Sherman,
New York, William H. Taft's Vice
President (1909); Mayor of Utica;
Representative in Congress;
renominated for Vice President in
1912 but died same year.

Thomas R. Marshall,
Indiana, Woodrow Wilson's Vice
President (1913); Governor of
Indiana, 1909–13 re-elected Vice
President, 1916; was 1912 choice of
Indiana Democratic delegation for
Presidency.

Calvin Coolidge,
Vermont and Massachusetts;
Warren G. Harding's Vice President
(1921); Massachusetts Governor
1919–20, succeeded to Presidency
1921.

Charles G. Dawes,
Ohio and Illinois; Calvin Coolidge's
Vice President (1925); held high
posts in World War I; utilities and
banking executive; lawyer; first
director Bureau of Budget.

Charles Curtis,
Kansas; Herbert C. Hoover's Vice
President (1929); Representative
and Senator; President pro tempore
Senate December 4–12, 1911,
Majority and Minority whip of
Senate, 1915–24.

John Nance Garner,
Texas; Franklin Delano Roosevelt's
Vice President (1933);
Representative to Congress and
Judge; Minority Leader and Speaker
of House; re-elected Vice President
1936.

Henry A. Wallace,
Iowa; FDR's Vice President (1941);
Editor, successful agricultural
experimentalist; Secretary of
Agriculture, 1933; Secretary of
Commerce, 1945–46.

Harry S. Truman,
Missouri, FDR's Vice President
(1945); Lieutenant, Captain and
Major, in World War I; Judge;
elected U.S. Senate, 1934;
re-elected, 1940; succeeded to
Presidency.

Alben W. Barkley,
Kentucky; Truman's Vice President
(1949); Judge; temporary Chairman,
Democratic National Conventions,
1932 and 1936; permanent, 1940.
Representative to Congress seven
terms; elected U.S. Senate four
times; Majority and Minority
Leader.

Richard Nixon,
California; Dwight D. Eisenhower's
Vice President (1953);
Representative and Senator;
Lieutenant-Commander World
War II; reelected Vice President,
1956; and elected President of U.S.
in 1968 and 1972.

Lyndon B. Johnson,
Texas; John F. Kennedy's Vice
President (1961); Representative
and Senator; public school teacher;
Lieutenant-Commander World
War II; Senate majority leader;
President.

Hubert H. Humphrey,
South Dakota and Minnesota;
Johnson's Vice President (1965);
pharmacist; instructor, political
science, University of Louisiana
and University of Minnesota;
Minneapolis Mayor; elected Senate,
1948, 1954, 1960 and 1970.

Spiro T. Agnew,
Maryland; Richard M. Nixon's Vice
President (1969, until resignation,
October 10, 1973); Governor of
Maryland, 1967–69.

Gerald R. Ford,
Nebraska and Michigan. Richard
Nixon's vice President from
December 6, 1973, until be became
President of the United States on
August 9, 1974. Former
Representative from Michigan
(1949–73) and House Minority
Leader (1965–73).

Nelson A. Rockefeller,
Maine and New York, former
Governor of New York
(1959–1973), inaugurated as the
41st Vice President of the United
States and President of the Senate
on December 19, 1974, before a live
television audience, marking the
first time the Senate permitted
television cameras. He served until
January 20, 1977.

Walter F. Mondale,
Minnesota; Carter's Vice President
(1976); former Minnesota Attorney
General, in 1964 appointed to U.S.
Senate to fill the unexpired term of
newly elected Vice President,
Hubert H. Humphrey; won election
to the Senate in 1966, and was
reelected in 1972. He served as Vice
President until January 20, 1981.

Pages of the United States Congress

Pages checking
legislative calendar.

The practice of employing pages to serve the Members of both the House and Senate, primarily as messengers, has evolved since the origin of the Federal government in 1789.

House pages are under the supervision of the Doorkeeper; Senate pages of the Sergeant at Arms. They deliver documents and messages and run errands for the Members. Visitors are intrigued by the bench pages who sit on the rostrum steps and assist the Members during the session. Others are assigned to the Cloakroom, the Speaker's office, and the Senate Majority and Minority Leaders.

Until 1971, only males were employed as pages. The first Senate female pages were appointed in May, 1971 by Senators Jacob Javits of New York and Charles Percy of Illinois. Former Speaker Carl Albert of Oklahoma appointed the first official female House page in 1973.

Pages are selected by the Senators or Representatives whose seniority permits this privilege. Senate pages may be between the ages of 14 and 17; House pages are limited to those who are 16 to 18, or who are juniors or seniors in high school. They must maintain at least a C average and be of good character. Pages live in rooming houses or with relatives in the area, since repeated efforts over the years have failed to provide a dormitory-education facility.

The pages attend the Capitol Page school currently located in the Library of Congress. They attend four or five 45-minute classes, five days a week, beginning at 6:10 a.m. and continuing until 9:45 a.m. The four year high school is accredited by the Middle States Association of Colleges and Secondary Schools. the curriculum is college preparatory, since 98 percent of the pages go on to college. There are six teachers and a principal-counselor, a basketball team, yearbook, school paper, student counsel and social and extra-curricular activities.

Numerous government officials, Members of the House of Representatives and Senate, officials of the House and Senate began their careers as Congressional pages. One incumbent Representative and one incumbent Senator are former pages: Representative John Dingell, Jr., of Michigan and Senator David H. Pryor of Arkansas.

A Senate page delivers
a document to Senator
Henry M. Jackson of
Washington.

Senator David H. Pryor
of Arkansas.

Representative John D.
Dingell of Michigan.

Pages receiving their assignments.

Pages on the steps of the Capitol.

Pages with the Speaker, Thomas P. O'Neill, Jr. of Massachusetts.

Graduation day for pages of the United States Congress.

Pages in the House cloakroom receiving instructions.

Pages sorting United States flags which flew over the Capitol.

Senate Democratic Leader Robert C. Byrd of West Virginia (right), with Walter (Joe) Stewart, Secretary to the Minority and pages in Senate cloakroom.

121

Your Congress at Work

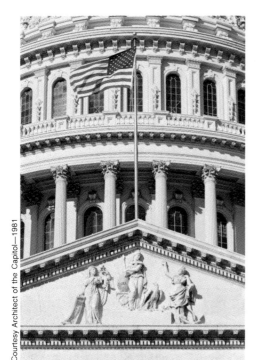

The East Central Pediment of the Capitol showing the marble carving "Genius of America."

A view of the Capitol by world renowned photographer Fred J. Maroon—taken from the Washington Monument.

97th Congress Profile

Members of Congress are as diverse as the States and districts they represent. They reflect the pluralistic nature of our society.

The "typical" Member of Congress is sometimes alluded to, but such a portrait gives a distorted view. The Congress is composed of five hundred and forty individuals from our 50 States, and the District of Columbia, Puerto Rico, Guam, the Virgin Islands and American Samoa, and each Member has a different personal history. Yet, as is true of the American people, Members of Congress share many traits, as this following summary indicates.

Age

When the 97th Congress convened in January 1981, the average age of its Members was 49.2, the youngest in at least 30 years. The average age of Members of the House of Representatives was 48.4, making it the youngest House since at least the 60th Congress (1907–1909). The average age of Members of the Senate was 52.5, making it the youngest Senate since at least the 45th Congress (1877–1879).

The youngest Representative is freshman John LeBoutillier, Republican of New York, who at 27 is one month younger than freshman John Hiler, Republican of Indiana, and two months younger than freshman Christopher Smith, Republican of New Jersey. The oldest Representative is Claude Pepper, Democrat of Florida, who is 80. Representatives must be at least 25 when they take office.

The youngest Senator is freshman Don Nickles, Republican of Oklahoma, who is 32. The oldest Senator is John Stennis, Democrat of Mississippi, who is 79. Senators must be at least 30 when they take office.

Father in the Senate, son in the House. The only father and son combination serving together in the Congress, Senator Barry M. Goldwater of Arizona and Representative Barry M. Goldwater, Jr., of California.

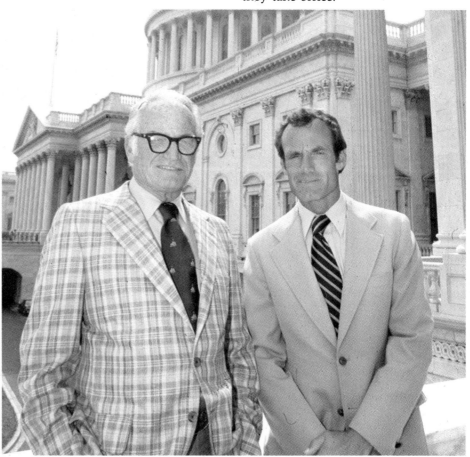

Occupations

As has been true in previous Congresses, law is the dominant profession in the 97th Congress although there has been a decline in the number of lawyer Members in the past four years. There are presently 255 Members who have listed law as their profession. In addition, there are 162 Members with a business or banking background; 68 educators; 37 Members with a farming or ranching background; 28 with a journalism background; seven engineers; four clergymen; four medical doctors; one dentist; one pharmacist; two optometrists and one Senator who is a veterinarian. There are at least 40 Members who are former Congressional staffers; two Senators who are former astronauts; and two Members who are former commercial airline pilots.

Representatives Philip M. Crane, left and Daniel B. Crane of Illinois, one of the two sets of brothers in the Congress.

Religion

During the last decade, the number of Members of Congress identifying with one religious denomination or another has remained well over 90 percent. More than 500 of the Members of the 97th Congress cite a specific religious affiliation.

Although Protestants of various denominations collectively hold more seats in the 97th Congress, Roman Catholics, with 136 in the two Houses, make up the largest contingent of any one denomination. Of the Protestants, there are 70 Methodists, 72 Episcopalians, 55 Presbyterians, 55 Baptists, and 20 Lutherans. There are also 31 Jewish Members of Congress and smaller numbers of members of other religious groups.

Education

The Members of the 96th Congress are highly educated. There are at least 332 Representatives and 80 Senators with bachelors degrees; 67 Representatives and 15 Senators with masters degrees; 196 Representatives and 60 Senators with law degrees; four Representatives, one Delegate, and one Senator with medical degrees; and 16 Representatives and four Senators with doctoral degrees.

Congressional Service

The average length of service of Representatives in the 97th Congress is 7.40 years, about three and one half terms. Representatives are elected for two-year terms. Representative Jamie Whitten, Democrat of Mississippi, has served longer in the House than any other Member of the 97th Congress. He is the Dean of the House and his service began on November 4, 1941.

Representative Claude Pepper of Florida. The only incumbent Member of Congress to have first served in the Senate and then the House.

The average length of service of Senators in the 97th Congress is 7.49 years, about one and one quarter terms. Senators are elected for six-year terms. Senator John Stennis, Democrat of Mississippi, has served longer in the Senate than any other Member of the 97th Congress. His service began on November 5, 1947.

Sex and Race

There are 20 women serving in the 97th Congress—two Senators and 18 Representatives. This is the highest number to serve in Congress; there were also 20 women who served in the 87th and 95th Congresses.

There are 18 black Members of the 97th Congress, all serving in the House of Representatives. This is the same as the record number of blacks who served in the 94th Congress.

There are also five Hispanic Members of the 97th Congress and five Members with an Oriental heritage.

Brothers, Representatives Phillip M. Burton, left and John L. Burton of California.

Women in American Politics

November 9, 1916 is a milestone in the history of the Nation. Miss Jeanette Rankin of Montana was elected as a bonafide member of the United States House of Representatives, nearly four years before most women were given the right to even vote. Representative Rankin was the first of 108 women who have been elected or appointed to Congress. Ninety-four other women have been elected to the House of Representatives, including nineteen in the 97th Congress. Fifteen women have served in the Senate, including two at the present time: Nancy Kassebaum of Kansas and Paula Hawkins of Florida. These two women also are the first elected to the Senate in their own right without having first been appointed or elected to fill an unexpired term of Members who resigned or died in office. Only five of the fifteen women who have served in the Senate have been elected to full six year terms; the other three are Hattie Caraway of Arkansas, Maurine Newberger of Oregon and Margaret Chase Smith of Maine. Senator Smith served six consecutive six-year terms, following four and a half terms in the House to which she was elected to succeed her husband who died in office.

Edith Nourse Rogers of Massachusetts holds the record for longevity of service by women in the House. She was elected to fill the vacancy caused by the death of her husband and served from June 25, 1925, until her death on September 10, 1960.

Courtesy of the Robert C. Cantrell Collection

Jeannette Rankin, an ardent suffragist, was elected to the 65th Congress in 1916, becoming the first woman Member of the House; and was elected again to the 77th Congress in 1941. Ironically, during her two separate terms, Congress declared war (1917 and 1941) and thus she became the only Representative to vote against both declarations.

Of the 44 women who first entered Congress before 1949, 57 percent were elected to fill another Member's unexpired term, and 43 percent were elected in a general election. Of the 59 women who first entered Congress after January 1949, 36 percent were chosen to fill vacancies, and 64 percent were elected in the general election. Forty-one percent of the women elected before 1949 succeeded their husbands in office, while only 25 percent of the women entering Congress after 1949 succeeded their husbands. Thus, since 1949, most of the women in Congress have been elected on their own for a full term.

Jeanette Rankin, an ardent suffragist and a woman of strong convictions, served twice in the House: during the 65th Congress (1917–1919) and again in the 77th Congress (1941–1943). Each time she voted against the declaration of war. In 1941 she was the only Member of Congress to do so.

Of the 15 women who have served in the Senate, Rebecca Felton of Georgia, who was appointed to the 67th Congress in 1922, holds at least two Senate records. She was the first female Senator, and at age 87, she was the oldest person ever to begin Senate service. Hattie Caraway of Arkansas was

Suffragists picket the White House. This passive scene, in January 1917, illustrates women's early fight for political equality.

The Sewell-Belmont House, home of the National Woman's Party, is located near the two newest Senate office buildings. It was declared a National Historic Site by act of Congress in 1975 in recognition of the women's suffrage movement.

During the War of 1812 the only shots fired against the British troops who burned the Capitol were fired from this house. Secretary of the Treasury Gallatin resided here during the development and signing of the Louisiana Purchase.

Visitors are welcomed each weekday from 10:00 a.m. to 2:00 p.m. and noon to 4:00 p.m. Saturday and Sunday.

Memorial to the Pioneers of the Women's Suffrage Movement.

This portrait monument of Elizabeth Cady Stanton, Susan B. Anthony and Lucretia Mott was accepted as a gift from the women of the United States, through the National Woman's Party, by the Joint Committee on the Library, February 15, 1921. The original block of marble from which these busts were carved measured 7'x5'8"x5', and the estimated weight is between 7 and 8 tons.

In accepting the monument the Joint Committee on the Library directed that it be placed temporarily "in the Rotunda for the purpose of appropriate ceremonies of tender and reception and at the conclusion of the ceremonies, the said sculpture be placed in the Crypt on the first floor of the Capitol beneath the Dome." It was moved from the Rotunda to the Crypt May 1921.

the first woman elected to a full six-year Senate term. She was appointed to the Senate in November 1931 to fill the vacancy caused by the death of her husband, and elected in January 1932 to fill the remainder of his term. She was reelected in 1938 and completed her service on January 3, 1945.

Representative Shirley Chisholm of New York is the first black woman to serve in Congress. She was first elected to the 91st Congress (1969–1971), and has been reelected ever since. Three other black women have been elected to Congress, all to the House of Representatives. They are: Cardiss Collins of Illinois, the former head of the Congressional Black Caucus, who began her service in the 93rd Congesss; and Barbara Jordan of Texas and Yvonne Burke of California, both of whom served in the 93d, 94th and 95th Congresses. Representative Burke also was

the first and only Member of Congress to give birth while in office. Her daughter was born during the 93rd Congress.

There are 20 women serving in the 97th Congress—two Senators and 18 Representatives. There had been a record number of 21 women elected to this Congress, but former Representative Gladys Spellman of Maryland was unable to take the oath of office because of illness and her seat was declared vacant. Twenty women also served in the 87th and 95th Congresses. Nineteen is the largest number of women to serve in the House at the same time. There were 19 women Representatives in the 94th Congress. Three is the largest number of women to serve in the Senate at the same time; there were three female Senators in both the 75th and 83rd Congresses.

Woman leaves jail after six day hunger strike in abandoned Occaquan work house after arrest on criminal charge of picketing White House.

Courtesy of the National Woman's Party.

Suffragists assemble with gold, purple and white banners for participation in voting rights parade near Capitol grounds, 1918.

Courtesy of the National Woman's Party.

The Congresswomen's Suite is located in the Capitol in what was at one time the Speaker's Office.

Pictured (left to right) seated are Representatives Marjorie S. Holt (Maryland); Geraldine A. Ferraro (New York); Barbara A. Mikulski (Maryland); Virginia Smith (Nebraska); Lindy Boggs (Louisiana).

Standing are Representatives Millicent Fenwick (New Jersey); Patricia Schroeder (Colorado); Margaret Heckler (Massachusetts); Marge Roukema (New Jersey); Shirley Chisholm (New York); Marilyn Lloyd Bouquard (Tennessee); Beverly B. Byron (Maryland).

Not pictured: Representatives Cardiss Collins (Illinois); Bobbi Fiedler (California); Lynn Martin (Illinois); Mary Rose Oakar (Ohio); Claudine Schneider (Rhode Island); Olympia J. Snowe (Maine).

Elected in 1978, Senator Nancy Landon Kassebaum, of Kansas, is the first woman elected to the United States Senate without having been preceded in Congress by a spouse or appointed to fill an unexpired term. She is the daughter of Alfred M. Landon, 1936 Republican presidential nominee and former Kansas Governor.

Senator Paula Hawkins, of Florida, was elected to the Senate on November 4, 1980. She serves on three committees— Agriculture, Nutrition, and Forestry; Labor and Human Resources and Joint Economic.

129

The Congress Represents You

Representative Norman Dicks listens carefully to an earnest constituent.

A student participating in Girl's Nation meets with Senator Bob Packwood of Oregon in his office.

Representative William L. Dickinson of Alabama, addressing thousands of farmers who came to Washington.

Television star Lorne Greene jokes with Representatives Bruce F. Vento of Minnesota and Ted Weiss of New York.

Summer interns pose with their sponsor, Senator Lowell P. Weicker, Jr. of Connecticut.

Senator Daniel K. Inouye of Hawaii talks with a group of students during one of his visits to the University of Hawaii campus in Honolulu.

Representative Ed Jones of Tennessee tours the Capitol area with constituents.

The younger generation makes a favorable impression on House Budget Committee Chairman James R. Jones of Oklahoma.

Representative Jack Brooks of Texas with a delegation from his district.

Senator John Melcher of Montana explains farm programs to students.

Senator Howard M. Metzenbaum of Ohio greets a group of young students during their tour to the Capitol.

Representative Margaret M. Heckler of Massachusetts (center), receives a memento from two 4-H Ambassadors.

Representative Ronald V. Dellums of California, left, and Representative Cardiss Collins of Illinois meet with Alex Haley author of *Roots* during his recent visit to the Capitol.

Senator John Tower of Texas (center), at a Washington reception for Texans.

Representative Richard C. Shelby of Alabama visits with friends.

Andrews Air Force Base is inspected by Representative Ferraro of New York

Senator Charles McC. Mathias, Jr., of Maryland (right), and Count Wilhem Wachtmeister, the Swedish Ambassador, participate in a Maryland Day wreath-laying ceremony in the Capitol.

Representative Claude Pepper of Florida receives visitors in his House office.

Senator Charles H. Percy of Illinois tries "pot luck" on a visit to his home state.

Senator Mack Mattingly of Georgia (far right) steps outside a committee room to meet with some visiting Georgians.

A visiting group hears Representative Jamie L. Whitten of Mississippi explain the congressional appropriations process.

Senator and Mrs. John W. Warner of Virginia greet the hostages returning from Iran.

Massachusetts matters are discussed by Representative Joe Moakley and a constituent.

Representative Carl D. Perkins of Kentucky greets a group on the House steps of the Capitol.

Senator Claiborne Pell of Rhode Island hears a constituent on the subject of support for the arts.

A high school band from Massachusetts is thanked by Senator Edward M. Kennedy after a concert on the Capitol steps.

Representative Augustus F. Hawkins of California welcomes two interns.

Former Senate Secretary J. Stanley Kimmitt (center) is honored as "third Senator from Montana" by Senator Max Baucus, Representative Ron Marlenee, Representative Pat Williams, and Senator John Melcher.

Representative Shirley Chisholm of New York explains the legislative process to young constituents.

House Majority Leader Jim Wright of Texas greets the astronauts and their wives.

A three-way discussion on the Capitol steps occupies Representatives Ed Bethune of Arkansas, Paul Simon of Illinois, and Thomas J. Downey of New York.

Senator Howell Heflin of Alabama and Representative David R. Bowen of Mississippi visit with Mr. and Mrs. Bill Simpson.

Senator Henry M. Jackson of Washington discusses his schedule with appointment secretary Dee Bartley.

Senator Max Baucus of Montana congratulates two recent participants in the Senate Youth Program from Montana.

Representative John D. Dingell of Michigan (right) explains his position on an issue to President Reagan, as Budget Director David Stockman and White House staff look on.

Representative Samuel S. Stratton of New York explains defense policy to students from his home state.

Representative John P. Hammerschmidt of Arkansas "lays out the picture" for a delegation from the state.

Representative and Mrs. Ron Marlenee of Montana (fourth and fifth from left) welcome Montanans to the Capitol.

Senator and Mrs. Alan Cranston chat with well known Washington restaurateurs Helen and Connie Valanos.

New York students listen attentively to their Representative, Peter A. Peyser.

Representative John L. Burton of California testifies for his constituents before a House Committee.

Representative James (Jimmy) H. Quillen checks the response to a questionnaire sent to his constituents in the 1st Congressional District of Tennessee.

President Reagan congratulates Senator Paul Laxalt upon completion of a speech.

Representatives Don H. Clausen of California (left) and Adam Benjamin, Jr. of Indiana (second from left) on House steps with constituents.

Representative Silvio O. Conte of Massachusetts poses with constituents representing three generations.

Senator Patrick J. Leahy of Vermont and his family welcome Jacques-Yves Cousteau to the Capitol.

Representatives Martin Frost of Texas, Michael D. Barnes of Maryland, and Howard Wolpe of Michigan with Iosif Mendelevich, dissident released from Soviet prison recently.

Representative Frank Horton greets the Richmond Family from the 34th Congressional District of New York.

Representative Lindy Boggs of Louisiana poses with Mardi Gras Queen and her attendant.

A town meeting in Kansas hears directly from their Representative Dan Glickman.

Presidential classroom students brief Representative Bill Frenzel of Minnesota, on their week-long activities.

Representative Floyd Spence of South Carolina and G. V. "Sonny" Montgomery pose with admirers—and vice versa.

135

The Committee System: Congress at Work

Members of the House Energy and Commerce Committee study the energy crisis situation.

Representatives Joseph M. Gaydos of Pennsylvania Chairman of the House Administration Subcommittee on Contracts and Printing and Newt Gingrich of Georgia listen to a witness.

"Congress in its committee rooms is Congress at work," wrote Woodrow Wilson. It is in the committees of Congress that bills undergo their closest scrutiny, that investigations—including oversight of the executive branch—are conducted, and that the differences in bills passed by each body are reconciled into one version acceptable to both.

Congress uses four different types of committees to perform these different functions: standing committees, select or special committees, joint committees and conference committees.

Committees that continue from Congress to Congress are called *standing committees.* The subject jurisdictions of these permanent committees are set forth in the Rules of each body, and virtually every introduced bill is referred to one or more of them according to the subjects involved. These are the committees that actually review proposed legislation and determine which bills shall be reported to each body.

In the 97th Congress, there are 22 standing committees in the House and 16 in the Senate. Most have several subcommittees with specific jurisdictions. Usually a standing committee sends a bill to one of its subcommittees for hearings, review and recommendations. The bill is then reported to the full committee for consideration. Finally, if approved by the full committee, the bill is reported to the full House or Senate.

Standing committees are also responsible for overseeing the operations of the executive departments and agencies under their respective jurisdictions. They usually perform this function by means of studies which provide Congress with the facts necessary to determine whether the agencies are administering legislation as intended. Congressional studies also help committees identify areas in which legislative action might be needed and the form that action might take.

Other Congressional studies are performed by *select* or *special committees.* Usually established for a limited period of time, these groups ordinarily deal with more specific subjects and issues than

Secretary of State Alexander Meigs Haig, Jr., during an appearance before the Senate Foreign Relations Committee for confirmation—photograph by Senator Howard H. Baker, Jr., of Tennessee.

do the standing committees. For example, in recent years each body has established a select or special committee on aging to study the multitude of problems that affect senior citizens.

Select committees of one body or the other have also studied population problems, narcotics, and Indian affairs. During the past decade each body has used a select committee to study its own committee system and to recommend improvements. Most select committees may investigate, study and make recommendations but may not report legislation. But both bodies have created a few permanent select committees in recent years and authorized them to report legislation.

Congress uses *joint committees* for investigatory and housekeeping purposes. These are usually permanent bodies composed of an equal number of House and Senate Members. Although in the past certain joint committees had the authority to consider and report legislation, no joint committee has that power in the 97th Congress. Usually joint committees are used to study broad and complex areas over a long period of time, an example being the Joint Economic Committee. Other joint committees, such as the Joint Committee on Printing, oversee functions connected with the operation of the legislative branch.

The last category of committees is the *conference committee.* These are formed to reconcile the differences between the

The Committee on House Administration, chaired by Representative Augustus F. Hawkins, of California, pauses for an official portrait in the Committee's hearing room.

The House Appropriations Committee's Subcommittee on the Legislative Branch hold hearings on Interior Department appropriations.

At a meeting of the Subcommittee on Rules of the House, Chairman John Joseph Moakley, of Massachusetts, confers with Representative Butler Derrick, of South Carolina.

Senators (from left) Paul Laxalt of Nevada; James A. McClure of Idaho; Lowell P. Weicker, Jr. of Connecticut, and Charles McC. Mathias, Jr. of Maryland during a mark up session.

Representative Marilyn Lloyd Bouquard of Tennessee Chairman of the House Subcommittee on Energy Research, confers with the Committee Counsel and the Assistant Counsel.

Chairman Richard Bolling of Missouri, presides at a meeting of House Rules Committee.

House Education and Labor Subcommittee on Health and Safety, Chairman Joseph M. Gaydos of Pennsylvania (right) and Committee Counsel Paul F. Dwyer.

Senator John Heinz, of Pennsylvania, and Representative Bill Frenzel of Minnesota, on the way to a House/Senate Conference committee.

The Senate Foreign Relations Committee, chaired by Senator Charles H. Percy of Illinois, conducts hearings on a Presidential appointment.

House and Senate when each passes a different version of the same bill. Conference committees are ad hoc joint committees, temporary panels appointed to deal with a single piece of legislation, dissolving upon the completion of that task. Members of both bodies serve on each conference committee, and the number of Members from each body may be the same. This is not as inequitable as it might seem because the voting in conference committees is by each body; its decisions must be approved by a majority of the Representatives and a majority of the Senators on the committee.

Every Member of the House serves on at least one standing committee except the Speaker and Minority Leader

The Joint Committee on Printing meets to review Committee rules and to select a Chairman and a Vice Chairman. Left to right are Representative Ed Jones of Tennessee; Representative Joseph Gaydos of Pennsylvania; Vice Chairman Augustus F. Hawkins, of California;

who, by tradition, serve on none. Senators must serve on at least two standing committees. In the House approximately 90 Representatives have only one committee assignment, usually because they sit on a particularly busy panel like Appropriations. All other House Members sit on two or three committees. In one way or another, both bodies limit the number of chairmanships any single Member may hold.

Committee sizes vary considerably and sometimes change from Congress to Congress. Because the House has more than four times as many Members as the Senate, its committees are generally larger. In the 97th Congress, the largest House committee—Appropriations—has 55 members, the largest Senate committee—also Appropriations—has 29. Most Senate standing committees have from 12 to 22 members, most House committees from 30 to 45. Traditionally, party ratios on committees correspond roughly to the party ratio in the full Chamber.

Committee and subcommittee service encourages Members to specialize in the subject areas of the panels on which they sit. Thus, the committee system continually builds up a reservoir of expertise to guide Congress as it attempts to deal with the Nation's needs.

Chairman Charles McC. Mathias, Jr. of Maryland; Senator John Warner of Virginia; and Representative Newt Gingrich of Georgia.

Not pictured: Senators Mark O. Hatfield of Oregon, Howard W. Cannon of Nevada, Wendell H. Ford of Kentucky, and Representative Lynn Martin of Illinois.

The Senate Committee on Rules and Administration, chaired by Senator Charles McC. Mathias, Jr. of Maryland.

Representatives William (Bill) Clay of Missouri (left), and Pat Williams of Montana during a meeting of the House Education and Labor Committee.

Senator Joseph R. Biden of Delaware questions a witness during a Senate Foreign Relations Committee hearing.

Senator Max Baucus of Montana takes notes during a meeting of the Senate Committee on Finance.

Representative Edward P. Boland of Massachusetts (second from left), Chairman of the House Permanent Select Committee on Intelligence and Representative C. W. Bill Young of Florida (second from right) confer with Committee staff during a hearing.

Speaker Thomas P. O'Neill, Jr. of Massachusetts appears before a House committee to testify in favor of emergency energy legislation.

Chairman Robert A. Roe of New Jersey (left) and John Paul Hammerschmidt of Arkansas confer during meeting of Subcommittee on Water Resources.

House Committee on Government Operations Chairman Jack Brooks of Texas calls the next witness.

House Appropriation Subcommittee on Labor, Health, Education and Welfare Members and Staff listen to witness.

Standing Committees
of the United States
Senate

Armed Services

Chairman,
John Tower
Texas

Ranking Minority
Member,
John C. Stennis
Mississippi

Agriculture,
Nutrition, and Forestry

Chairman,
Jesse Helms
North Carolina

Ranking Minority
Member,
Walter "Dee"
Huddleston
Kentucky

Banking,
Housing, and Urban Affairs

Chairman,
Jake Garn
Utah

Ranking Minority
Member,
Harrison A. Williams, Jr.
New Jersey

Appropriations

Chairman,
Mark O. Hatfield
Oregon

Ranking Minority
Member,
William Proxmire
Wisconsin

Budget

Chairman,
Pete V. Domenici
New Mexico

Ranking Minority
Member,
Ernest F. Hollings
South Carolina

Commerce, Science, and Transportation

Chairman,
Bob Packwood
Oregon

Ranking Minority
Member,
Howard W. Cannon
Nevada

Foreign Relations

Chairman,
Charles H. Percy
Illinois

Ranking Minority
Member,
Claiborne Pell
Rhode Island

Rules and Administration

Chairman,
Charles
McC. Mathias, Jr.
Maryland

Ranking Minority
Member,
Wendell H. Ford
Kentucky

Energy and Natural Resources

Chairman,
James A. McClure
Idaho

Ranking Minority
Member,
Henry M. Jackson
Washington

Governmental Affairs

Chairman,
William V. Roth, Jr.
Delaware

Ranking Minority
Member,
Thomas F. Eagleton
Missouri

Small Business

Chairman,
Lowell P. Weicker, Jr.
Connecticut

Ranking Minority
Member,
Sam Nunn
Georgia

Environment and Public Works

Chairman,
Robert T. Stafford
Vermont

Ranking Minority
Member,
Jennings Randolph
West Virginia

Judiciary

Chairman,
Strom Thurmond
South Carolina

Ranking Minority
Member,
Joseph R. Biden, Jr.
Delaware

Veterans' Affairs

Chairman,
Alan K. Simpson
Wyoming

Ranking Minority
Member,
Alan Cranston
California

Finance

Chairman,
Robert J. Dole
Kansas

Ranking Minority
Member,
Russell B. Long
Louisiana

Labor and Human Resources

Chairman,
Orrin G. Hatch
Utah

Ranking Minority
Member,
Edward M. Kennedy
Massachusetts

141

Select and Special Committees of the United States Senate

Aging

Chairman,
John Heinz
Pennsylvania

Ranking Minority
Member,
Lawton Chiles
Florida

Indian Affairs

Chairman,
William S. Cohen
Maine

Ranking Minority
Member,
John Melcher
Montana

Ethics

Chairman,
Malcolm Wallop
Wyoming

Vice Chairman,
Howell Heflin
Alabama

Intelligence

Chairman,
Barry Goldwater
Arizona

Vice Chairman,
Daniel Patrick
Moynihan
New York

Standing Committees of the United States House of Representatives

Appropriations

Chairman,
Jamie L. Whitten
Mississippi

Ranking Minority
Member,
Silvio O. Conte
Massachusetts

Banking, Finance and Urban Affairs

Chairman,
Fernand J. St Germain
Rhode Island

Ranking Minority
Member,
J. William Stanton
Ohio

Agriculture

Chairman,
E (Kika) de la Garza
Texas

Ranking Minority
Member,
William C. Wampler
Virginia

Armed Services

Chairman,
Melvin Price
Illinois

Ranking Minority
Member,
William L. Dickinson
Alabama

Budget

Chairman,
James R. Jones
Oklahoma

Ranking Minority
Member,
Delbert L. Latta
Ohio

District of Columbia

Chairman,
Ronald V. Dellums
California

Ranking Minority
Member,
Stewart B. McKinney
Connecticut

Government Operations

Chairman,
Jack Brooks
Texas

Ranking Minority
Member,
Frank Horton
New York

Merchant Marine and Fisheries

Chairman,
Walter B. Jones
North Carolina

Ranking Minority
Member,
Gene Snyder
Kentucky

Education and Labor

Chairman,
Carl D. Perkins
Kentucky

Ranking Minority
Member,
John M. Ashbrook
Ohio

House Administration

Chairman,
Augustus F. Hawkins
California

Ranking Minority
Member,
Bill Frenzel
Minnesota

Post Office and Civil Service

Chairman,
William D. Ford
Michigan

Ranking Minority
Member,
Edward J. Derwinski
Illinois

Energy and Commerce

Chairman,
John D. Dingell
Michigan

Ranking Minority
Member,
James T. Broyhill
North Carolina

Interior and Insular Affairs

Chairman,
Morris K. Udall
Arizona

Ranking Minority
Member,
Manuel Lujan, Jr.
New Mexico

Public Works and Transportation

Chairman,
James J. Howard
New Jersey

Ranking Minority
Member,
Don H. Clausen
California

Foreign Affairs

Chairman,
Clement J. Zablocki
Wisconsin

Ranking Minority
Member,
Wm. S. Broomfield
Michigan

Judiciary

Chairman,
Peter W. Rodino, Jr.
New Jersey

Ranking Minority
Member,
Robert McClory
Illinois

Rules

Chairman,
Richard Bolling
Missouri

Ranking Minority
Member,
James H. Quillen
Tennessee

Standing Committees of the United States House of Representatives

continued

Small Business

Chairman,
Parren J. Mitchell
Maryland

Ranking Minority
Member,
Joseph M. McDade
Pennsylvania

Veterans' Affairs

Chairman,
G. V. (Sonny)
Montgomery
Mississippi

Ranking Minority
Member,
John Paul
Hammerschmidt
Arkansas

Science and Technology

Chairman,
Don Fuqua
Florida

Ranking Minority
Member,
Larry Winn, Jr.
Kansas

Standards of Official Conduct

Chairman,
Louis Stokes
Ohio

Ranking Minority
Member,
Floyd Spence
South Carolina

Ways and Means

Chairman,
Dan Rostenkowski
Illinois

Ranking Minority
Member,
Barber B. Conable, Jr.
New York

Select and Special Committees of the United States House of Representatives

Aging

Chairman,
Claude Pepper
Florida

Ranking Minority
Member,
Matthew J. Rinaldo
New Jersey

Intelligence

Chairman,
Edward P. Boland
Massachusetts

Ranking Minority
Member,
J. Kenneth Robinson
Virginia

Narcotics Abuse and Control

Chairman,
Leo C. Zeferetti
New York

Ranking Minority
Member,
Tom Railsback
Illinois

Joint Committees of the United States Congress

Economic

Chairman,
Representative
Henry S. Reuss
Wisconsin

Vice Chairman,
Senator
Roger W. Jepsen
Iowa

Printing

Chairman,
Senator Charles
McC. Mathias, Jr.
Maryland

Vice Chairman,
Representative
Augustus F. Hawkins
California

Library

Chairman,
Representative
Augustus F. Hawkins
California

Vice Chairman,
Senator Charles
McC. Mathias, Jr.
Maryland

Taxation

Chairman,
Representative
Dan Rostenkowski
Illinois

Vice Chairman,
Senator
Robert J. Dole
Kansas

Two Committee Rooms
of the Congress.

Revenue and Appropriations

Collecting and spending money are basic and crucial governmental powers. Under our Constitution the executive branch carries out these responsibilities, but within limits established by Congress.

The government collects its revenues through taxes, excises, duties, customs and the sale of bonds, among other means. These monies pay for the operation of the Federal Government and the financing of Federal programs.

Article I, Section 8, of the Constitution declares that "The Congress shall have Power To lay and collect Taxes, Duties, Imposts, and Excises, to pay the Debts and provide for the common Defence and general Welfare of the United States; . . ." Thus, the Congress, not the President, is empowered to impose taxes. When the Founding Fathers wrote this section of the Constitution, the memory of outrageous actions by colonial Governors was still

The Senate Committee on Appropriations, chaired by Senator Mark O. Hatfield, of Oregon, meets in the beautiful committee room located in S–128 of the Capitol.

fresh in their minds. They were determined to prevent the Executive from laying arbitrary taxes on the people. Thus, Article I, Section 7, of the Constitution states that "All Bills for raising Revenue shall originate in the House of Representatives; but the Senate may propose or concur with Amendments as on other Bills."

Under their respective rules, the responsibility for drafting tax laws lies with the Ways and Means Committee in the House and the Finance Committee in the Senate. Because their decisions directly and significantly affect the Nation's economy and the lives of virtually all Americans, these two committees are considered to be among the most powerful in Congress.

Federal agencies and departments spend money under the terms of appropriation laws enacted by Congress. These laws specify how much may be spent for each government program and activity during a stated period of time, usually one year. As with revenue measures, the Constitution gives the appropriation powers to Congress. Article I, Section 9 states: "No Money shall be drawn from the Treasury, but in Consequence of Appropriations made by Law; and a regular Statement and Account of the Receipts and Expenditures of all public Money shall be published from time to time." By loosening the government's purse strings or by pulling them tighter, Congress can compel executive agencies to increase or decrease their spending and thereby determine the scope of their activities.

Although the Constitution does not explicitly empower the House to initiate appropriation bills, the House does so by custom. The Senate, as with revenue and all other measures sent to it by the House, may amend appropriation bills, increasing or decreasing amounts and inserting items of appropriation on its own initiative.

The Appropriations Committees of each House are vested with primary responsibility for recommending spending amounts. Not surprisingly, these committees are also generally ranked among the most powerful in Congress.

At one time, the revenue and appropriations committees made just about all the important decisions on raising and spending money. Today their decisions, although still crucial, are part of a complex budget process involving the legislative or authorizing committees as well as the executive branch.

House Ways and Means Committee Members, (left to right) Representatives Charles B. Rangel, of New York; J. J. Pickle, of Texas; Sam Gibbons, of Florida; Chairman Dan Rostenkowski, of Illinois; Ranking Minority Member Barber B. Conable, Jr., of New York and Representative John J. Duncan, of Tennessee, listen intently to testimony presented during a Committee meeting.

Secretary of the Treasury Donald T. Regan visits with Members of the Senate Finance Committee prior to a hearing.

147

Revenue, appropriations and budget decisions made by these twelve Members of Congress and the six committees they lead touch the pocketbook of every American.

House Appropriations Committee

Representative Jamie Whitten, of Mississippi, Chairman.

Representative Silvio Conte, of Massachusetts, Ranking Minority Member.

House Committee on Budget

Representative James R. Jones, of Oklahoma, Chairman.

Representative Delbert L. Latta, of Ohio, Ranking Minority Member.

House Ways and Means Committee

Representative Dan Rostenkowski, of Illinois, Chairman.

Representative Barber B. Conable, Jr., of New York, Ranking Minority Member.

Senate Finance Committee

Senator Robert Dole, of Kansas, Chairman.

Senator Russell B. Long, of Louisiana, Ranking Minority Member.

Senate Appropriations Committee

Senator Mark O. Hatfield, of Oregon, Chairman.

Senator William Proxmire, of Wisconsin, Ranking Minority Member.

Senate Budget Committee

Senator Pete V. Domenici, of New Mexico, Chairman.

Senator Ernest F. Hollings, of South Carolina, Ranking Minority Member.

Senate Budget Committee Chairman Pete V. Domenici of New Mexico (right) and Ranking Minority Member Ernest F. Hollings of South Carolina during a markup session of the Senate Budget Committee.

Until recently Congress had no mechanisms for considering the budget in an integrated way. Each committee focused solely on its parts of the budget and brought those parts to the floor of its House for separate action. Neither the Congress nor any of its committees ever put the parts together to consider the budget as a whole, to compare the total revenue and spending amounts, to calculate the resulting surplus or deficit, or to determine whether such a surplus or deficit was desirable. Nor did Congress or any of its committees ever consider overall spending priorities: what proportion of the government's resources should go to defense, to social programs, to agriculture, and so forth. By default, Congress left these concerns to the President.

Many Members of Congress, and others, believed that the legislature was evading its responsibilities by clinging to this approach. They argued that Congress, lacking the means for developing alternatives to the President's budget, was reduced to mere tinkering with its details.

Congress responded to these criticisms in 1974 by enacting the Congressional Budget and Impoundment Control Act. This Act created a Budget Committee in each House to examine the budget as a whole, to review spending priorities, and to suggest alternatives to the President's budget proposals. A non-partisan Congressional Budget Office was established to provide Congress with budgetary information and analyses. A new procedure was set up to give Congress the opportunity to consider the budget as a whole, and a timetable was adopted to encourage the timely enactment of authorization and appropriation bills.

Since 1921 the law has required the President to take the first step in this process: preparing and submitting to Congress in each January his budget recommendations for the entire government. Then Congress takes over.

It sends tax proposals to the revenue committees, spending proposals to the appropriations committees, and legislative proposals to the authorizing committees. The authorizing committees recommend policies and activities while the appropriations committees recommend spending amounts. Under the rules of both Houses, bills authorizing the existence of many government agencies and activities must be acted on before appropriations for them may be considered.

Under the new arrangements, each Budget Committee reviews the President's budget plus recommendations from all other committees early in the year. By April 15 the Budget Committees must report a concurrent resolution embodying their recommendations for overall budget amounts and for spending in all of the major functional categories. Congress is supposed to complete its consideration of this first budget resolution by May 15. The purpose of the first budget resolution is to set targets for Congress and its committees as the individual parts of the budget come up for consideration.

Between May and September Congress must enact all of its spending bills. By September 15 it must agree to a second concurrent budget resolution, also reported by the Budget Committees, revising or affirming the first resolution figures.

In either budget resolution Congress may direct committees to reduce spending in legislation within their jurisdictions. Such directions are known as reconciliation instructions and the measure implementing these instructions, a reconciliation bill or resolution. Congress must complete reconciliation action by September 25.

Once Congress completes action on the second budget resolution and reconciliation measure (if required), it may not consider any spending legislation that would exceed the levels of the second resolution.

The House Appropriations Committee for the 97th Congress.

Chairman James R. Jones, of Oklahoma (left), and Ranking Minority Member Delbert L. Latta, of Ohio (right), during a markup session of the House Budget Committee. Committee Executive Director Mace Broide stands in the rear.

Congress in International Affairs

Sir Winston Churchill, Prime Minister of Great Britain, addresses a Joint Meeting, May, 1943.

The expanded role of Congress in foreign affairs in the seventies has resulted in vastly increased contacts between the Congress and foreign dignitaries visiting the United States. The House Foreign Affairs Committee, under the Chairmanship of Clement J. Zablocki of Wisconsin, and the Senate Foreign Relations Committee, under the Chairmanship of Charles H. Percy of Illinois,

take the lead in welcoming these dignitaries to the Capitol and United States Congress.

The Congress of the United States is a leading and influential participant in these interparliamentary meetings, where discussions and policy resolutions are aimed at improving world amity, peace, and the free exchange of people and ideas.

The oldest formally organized interparliamentary body is the Interparliamentary Union, established in 1889, to which all nations claiming to have parliamentary forms of government may apply for membership. The total number of nations varies from year to year but averages about 75, including several of the Eastern bloc countries. The group meets twice annually, in the spring and in the fall, with each meeting held in a different country.

The North Atlantic Treaty Organization Parliamentarians' Conference (later renamed the North Atlantic Assembly) was formed in 1955. United States participation was authorized in Public Law 689, 84th Congress, 2d Session, approved on July 11, 1956.

The North Atlantic Assembly holds an annual plenary session each autumn in one of the NATO countries. Com-

House Majority Leader Jim Wright has the attention of Great Britain's Prime Minister Margaret Thatcher and House Foreign Affairs Chairman Zablocki.

Speaker O'Neill and House Foreign Affairs Chairman Clement J. Zablocki of Wisconsin watch as Robert Mugabe, Prime Minister of Zimbabwe, signs the guest book.

mittees of the Assembly meet throughout the year. In 1980 Representative Jack Brooks of Texas was elected President of the Assembly.

The Canada-United States Interparliamentary Group was established by Congress under Public Law 86–42. Senator Ted Stevens of Alaska and Representative Dante Fascell of Florida served as Cochairmen for the Twenty-second Canada-United States Interparliamentary Conference in Canada in 1981.

The Mexico-United States Interparliamentary Group was established under Public Law 86–420. Beginning in 1961, annual conferences have been held in the United States in even-numbered years and in Mexico in odd-numbered years. Senator Charles H. Percy of Illinois and Representative E de la Garza of Texas served as Cochairmen for the Twenty-first Mexico-United States Interparliamentary Conference, held in Mexico in June, 1981, with Majority Leader James Wright of Texas as ex-officio Chairman.

In addition to the above-mentioned interparliamentary groups which are specifically authorized and established by Congressional resolutions, a number of regular exchanges take place on a less formalized basis—under the general aegis of the House Committee on Foreign Affairs, the Senate Committee on Foreign Relations, and the leadership of both Houses of Congress. Numerous ad hoc parliamentary delegations from many nations are received and frequently confer with Committees and their staffs, or with individual Members. In turn, Senators and Representatives are invited by foreign governments' parliamentary bodies to exchange ideas in search of greater international understanding which is essential to world peace.

Senator and Mrs. Joseph R. Biden, of Delaware, during an audience with His Holiness John Paul II at the Vatican.

Vice Premier Deng Xiao Ping, of the People's Republic of China, joins in the applause at a tea meeting in his honor. Also among those present are House Majority Leader James C. Wright of Texas and Speaker Thomas P. O'Neill of Massachusetts. January, 1979.

United States Ambassador to Japan Mike Mansfield catches up on Montana news with Senator Max Baucus of Montana.

Senator John W. Warner, of Virginia, welcomes West German Chancellor Helmut Schmidt to the Capitol as Senators William S. Cohen, of Maine (right), and Rudy Boschwitz, of Minnesota, look on.

151

A delegation from the Supreme Soviet of the U.S.S.R., headed by Boris N. Ponomarev, began a 10-day visit to the United States with this official luncheon. Speaker Thomas P. O'Neill of Massachusetts is seated at the left, and House Foreign Affairs Committee Chairman Clement J. Zablocki of Wisconsin stands at the right. January, 1978.

Israel's Prime Minister Menachem Begin and Senator Claiborne Pell greet each other with warmth.

His Holiness John Paul II addresses Members of Congress on his October 1979 visit to the Nation's Capitol.

Senator Claiborne Pell of Rhode Island, Prime Minister Zenko Suzuki of Japan and Senate Foreign Relations Chairman Charles Percy of Illinois discuss a mutual concern at lunch.

President Anwar Sadat of the Arab Republic of Egypt at a ceremonial reception which marked the signing of a peace treaty between his nation and the State of Israel, in March, 1979. With him are House Majority Leader James C. Wright of Texas, Speaker Thomas P. O'Neill of Massachusetts, House Minority Leader John J. Rhodes of Arizona and House Foreign Affairs Committee Chairman Clement J. Zablocki of Wisconsin.

His Excellency, Julius K. Nyerere, President of the United Republic of Tanzania, with the late Senator Humphrey of Minnesota, the late Representative Leo J. Ryan of California.

152

His Excellency the late Masayoshi Ohira Prime Minister of Japan with Speaker Thomas P. O'Neill.

The Honorable Armando Sanchez Bueno, President of the Venezuelan Chamber of Deputies signs in as Chairman Zablocki looks on.

Mayor Jacques Chirac of Paris, France, addressing the members of the North Atlantic Assembly. At left, Representative Jack Brooks of Texas, the President of the Assembly.

From the Assembly of the Azores, President Alvaro Monjardino in conversation with Portuguese Ambassador João Hail Themido and Senator Claiborne Pell of Rhode Island.

His Excellency Francesco Cossiga (center), President of the Council of Ministers of the Italian Republic with Representatives Peter W. Rodino, Jr. and Clement J. Zablocki.

Senator Henry Jackson of Washington is briefed by Under Secretary of State for Security Assistance James Buckley.

The Modern Congress

Congress in the last decade has continued the traditions and customs developed over the past 200 years; at the same time, however, it has demonstrated that Congress is an adaptable institution. During this past decade not only has the membership changed but also, where there were compelling reasons, methods and procedures have been modified. New technology and management practices were adopted where feasible and Senators and Representatives began a major effort to keep themselves, and their staffs, better informed. Actions taken at the beginning of the 97th Congress continued this movement and these changes, as well as those proposed for the early eighties, will insure a modern Congress configured to meet the challenges now faced by the American people and their elected leaders.

During consideration by the Senate Committee on Rules and Administration of a resolution providing for the televising of Senate floor debate, Senate Majority Leader Howard H. Baker, Jr., of Tennessee, testifies in favor of the proposal.

Courtesy Alan E. Porter—Senate Photographic Studio.

Background

The House Chamber, a blending of old and new, dramatizes the fact that the Congress is a living institution.

Congress is a living, dynamic institution. Sometimes slowly, sometimes rapidly, Congressional membership, organization and procedures constantly change under the impact of the shifting economic, political and social circumstances of the nation. As one scholar has put it, Congress is in a perpetual state of reform. Even so, the pace of Congressional change was unusually rapid in the 1970s and thus in the 1980s the institution is different in many significant ways from what it was a decade ago.

The fundamental Congressional framework has changed very little. The basic constitutional structure and powers of Congress have been little altered since the House of Representatives and the Senate first convened in 1789. Representatives are still elected to two-year terms and Senators to six-year terms, for example, although Senators are now directly chosen by the people instead of by State legislatures as they were before 1914. Both Houses still maintain a system of standing committees to study bills on particular subjects and recommend whether they should become law, and some of those committees have existed continuously since the early 19th century. Most of the basic rules and procedures developed in the last century for debating and amending bills on the floors of the House and the Senate are still used today. The two Houses continue to apply the same means for reconciling their differences on legislation and for monitoring how the executive branch interprets and enforces acts of Congress.

The Senate Recording Studio assists Senators in the informing of their constituents of legislative issues by video-taping their statements and interviews for subsequent broadcasting. Senator Wendell H. Ford, of Kentucky is being taped by staff of the Recording Studio using mini-cameras on the Capitol lawn.

157

Moreover, the number of individuals each Member represents has grown enormously. Between 1800 and 1980 the average population in House districts rose from about 34,000 to more than 517,000. Also, as late as 1962 the actual populations of Congressional districts varied widely, in some instances by as much as 800,000 people. Supreme Court decisions of the mid-1960s corrected that inequity; today district population sizes are as nearly equal as possible, given the constitutional requirement that every State must have at least one Representative no matter how small its population. The sharp increases in the number of people represented have been accompanied in recent decades by rising constituent demands for additional services from their Representatives and Senators, considerably expanding each legislator's workload. This growth has contributed to the pressure for expanded staff and physical space on Capitol Hill.

On the other hand, long-term national population shifts have profoundly affected the composition of Congress and the work of its Members. The size of the House has increased from only 65 in the First Congress to the present total of 435, plus Delegates from the District of Columbia, Guam, the Virgin Islands, and American Samoa, and the Resident Commissioner from Puerto Rico. The Senate also expanded as new States entered the Union.

Furthermore, as more Americans have moved from rural to urban areas the number of city and suburban Congressional districts has increased while that of predominately farming districts has declined. At the same time significant population shifts from frostbelt to sunbelt States have inexorably brought more House seats to the south, southwest and west at the expense of the northeast and midwest.

From time to time both Houses of Congress have significantly altered their rules and procedures. During the 19th century the minority in the House of Representatives acquired inordinate powers of obstruction. That trend was decisively reversed in 1890 under the leadership of Speaker Thomas B. Reed. From that time forward both parties have accepted the principle that, while protecting legitimate minority rights, the rules of the House must not prevent the majority from enacting its legislative proposals. Shortly after the turn of the century the House curtailed the powers of its Speaker, removing him from the chairmanship of the powerful Rules Committee and stripping him of the power to appoint all committee chairmen and members. A few years later the Senate adopted its first permanent cloture procedure to limit filibusters.

Other piecemeal changes continued to be made until 1946, when the Congress enacted a comprehensive Legislative Reorganization Act. Among its other achievements, this milestone of recent Congressional history sharply reduced the number of House and Senate committees, improved committee procedures, authorized professional staff for all committees, strengthened Congressional research agencies, modified the appropriations process, shifted responsibility for settling minor claims against the government to executive agencies and the courts, thereby considerably reducing the minor items in the workload of Congress, and formally established oversight of the executive branch as a continuing statutory responsibility of the legislature.

THE CONGRESSIONAL STAFF JOURNAL
STAFF

Hill Tries Its New Information Aids

Data on Geographic Basis

One evening just about a year ago a Congressional committee aide was watching a popular investigative-news television program and becoming increasingly curious about various aspects of some of the Federal funding discussed in the show.

The next morning he called a familiar "downtown" source for information on some of the matters that were nagging at his professional curiosity, only to be informed that the facts he wanted were probably already available through a then-new operation right on the Hill.

As a result, he called the Program and Budget Division of House Information Systems (H.I.S.) for the data he wanted and thereby, unwittingly, became the first non-test-period customer of

(Continued on page 18)

Schedules, Updates, Other Facts

The cliche lingers, making the name of the United States Senate almost synonymous with the words "deliberative body."

Time was, however, and not too long ago, when most Senators and their staffs were hard put to find out which of their colleagues were deliberating about what subjects at any given time.

With the beginning of the present session of the 96th Congress, that changed.

Now, as a result of expansion to the Senate's computer system capabilities, Senators and their aides can, on a normal morning, determine immediately at their computer terminals which committees and subcommittees are scheduled to be meeting as well as the names of the Senators

(Continued on page 2)

Need a room for an official meeting? See pages 12 and 13.

The *Congressional Staff Journal* provides useful information to the staffs of the Senate, embracing a broad range of articles on professional activities and interests.

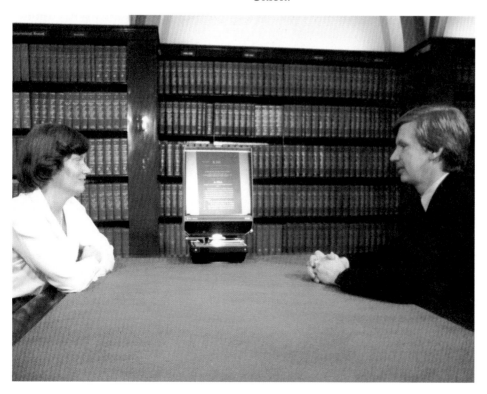

Assistant Secretary of the Senate, Marilyn Courtot, and Deputy Senate Sergeant at Arms, Larry Smith, are using a microfilm viewer in the Senate Library for researching legislation of prior Congresses.

During the two decades that followed, Congress absorbed, modified, and considered the consequences of the 1946 Act. By reducing the number of committees and expanding the breadth of subjects under the jurisdiction of each, the Act had enhanced the influence of their chairmen. The stature of these powerful figures was further strengthened by invariable adherence to the seniority system which virtually guaranteed chairmanships to the committees' most senior majority party members. Following the consolidation of the committees, the number of subcommittees grew rapidly in both Houses. In the Senate, periodic battles erupted over proposals to strengthen cloture and the rule was twice modified. The House adopted rules to protect the rights of witnesses appearing before investigating committees and took steps to give the majority party's leadership greater influence over the Rules Committee.

Into the 1980s

The momentum for a new surge of Congressional change began to build in the mid-1960s. In 1965 both Houses agreed to the creation of a joint committee to restudy the whole structure and operation of the legislative branch and to make comprehensive recommendations. Many of these were incorporated into the Legislative Reorganization Act of 1970 which inaugurated a decade of numerous and far-reaching changes in almost every major feature of the legislature. Much of the impetus for this reform activity was supplied by the unusually large new generation of legislators that flooded into Congress in the 1970s. By 1979 two-thirds of the Representatives and about three-fifths of the Senators had served in their respective Houses only since 1970.

The power and influence of committee chairmen received particular attention during the 1970s. The 1970 Act gave committee Members a larger voice in committee proceedings. During the next several years, party caucuses eased the rigidity of the seniority system by making the appointment of chairmen subject to biennial election. In the House, committee chairmen lost control over the organization, membership, jurisdictions, and staff of subcommittees. Furthermore, both Houses adopted rules that distributed chairmanships and committee seats more widely among their Members.

Committee jurisdiction was another subject of deep concern. Unforeseen in 1946, the emergence of such new national problems as energy, environmental protection, occupational safety and health care strained the ability of the committee system to produce coordinated and comprehensive policies. The 1970 Act made a few minor changes in the Senate's system; major alterations were agreed to in 1977. The House modified its system somewhat in 1974 and appointed a select committee to restudy the situation in 1979.

Publications about activities and offices of the Congress assist Members, staff, and the public in better understanding functions of the Congress.

Congressional staff use a variety of computer terminals in their offices for accessing retrieval systems and performing word processing. Computers and terminals are connected to cable networks installed by staff of the Architect of the Capitol.

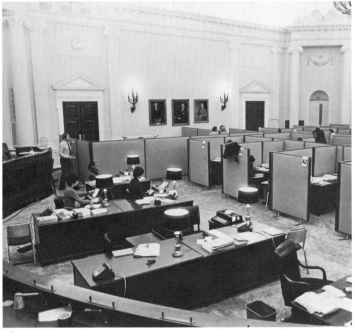

Increased demands on Members of Congress have necessitated early organization of both bodies. Temporary partitions were set up in the Committee on Ways and Means hearing room for use by House Members in interviewing prospective staff to perform the many technical, secretarial, and professional tasks which constituents expect of their Members.

Both Houses took steps to speed up the legislative process in the 1970s. In the Senate it became the normal practice to consider almost every important bill under unanimous consent agreements that limited debate. To cope with situations in which such agreements could not be concluded, the Senate repeatedly strengthened its cloture rule; in 1975, 1976, and again in 1979. Meanwhile the House was amending its rules to restrict delaying tactics and to increase the use of procedures for expeditious consideration of legislation.

Major strides were taken during the 1970s to open the workings of Congress to the public view and to improve communications between Members and their constituents. Before this decade most committee meetings were held behind closed doors. Today, with few exceptions, committee meetings and hearings are conducted "in the sunshine," to promote better public understanding of national issues and proposals for responding to them. Committees may now permit radio and television coverage of their activities; the Senate has experimented with radio broadcasts of its floor debates; and the House has begun to televise its floor debates.

Votes that once went unrecorded are now a matter of public record, and the Congressional Record has been made a more accurate transcript of Congressional proceedings. New facilities and technologies have been developed to enable Representatives and Senators to explain their views and actions to their constituents, both from Washington and while at home. And Congress has adopted new codes of financial disclosure and standards of conduct.

As the issues facing Congress grew in number and complexity, the legislature expanded its resources. Congressional staffs were enlarged to assist Members and committees in formulating policies and reviewing their implementation. Major new research and analysis responsibilities were assigned to the General Accounting Office and to the Congressional Research Service of the Library of Congress. The Congressional Budget Office was established to provide expert information on national economic trends and their implications for Congressional spending and taxing decisions. An Office of Technology Assessment was created to analyze the impact of technological developments on present and future public policies.

Congress also took several major steps to reassert its great constitutional powers during the 1970s. In 1973, for example, the legislature adopted the War Powers Resolution, which clarified the respective roles of the President and the Congress in cases of threatened or undeclared hostilities. The Congressional Budget and Impoundment Control Act was passed in the following year to provide Congress with a better procedure for establishing spending priorities and improving the coordination of spending and taxing policies.

Clearly Congress must and will continue to change. In no other way can it remain a vital and responsive instrument of democratic government. But the history of the institution reveals an underlying continuity, a devotion to the constitutional framework within which it was created. If the past is a reliable guide to the future, Congress will continue to confine its ceaseless evolution within the bounds of that stable and tested framework.

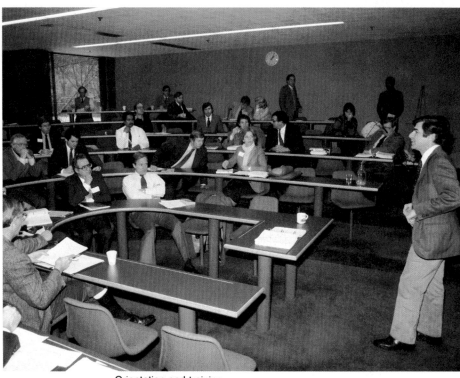

Orientation and training for new Members includes workshops and seminars on Capitol Hill and elsewhere. This class is being conducted at the Harvard Seminar for new Members of the House of Representatives.

Information about Committee meetings, hearings, and mark-up sessions is entered into the Legis System by staff of the Senate Daily Digest Office for computer retrieval.

Technology in Congress

As the issues confronting the Nation have grown more complex. The Congress has become an increasingly demanding environment where legislation, committee activities and constituent interests vie for Members' time and attention. These trends led Congress to look for new approaches to traditional tasks.

Modern computers, telecommunications, microforms and audio-video devices, as well as the associated new information management techniques, have proved to be valuable aids in administrative operations as well as for research and analysis. There is continuing interest in exploring new avenues for improving the efficiency of Congressional operations and enhancing the quality of information available to legislators. To meet this demand, the House, Senate and the Library of Congress now have professional staffs and sophisticated machine capabilities supporting the introduction and maintenance of needed technical services.

Budget and Policy Analysis

A broad spectrum of budget analysis and monitoring projects have been developed to support the House and Senate Committees on the Budget, Appropriations, Finance, and Ways and Means, the Congressional Budget Office and House and Senate authorizing committees since the passage of the Congressional Budget and Impoundment Control Act of 1974. Computer services are now available for committees and offices involved in budget formulation, analysis and tracking which show the impact that specific legislation can have on the total budget.

A "fisheye" view of one of the data processing centers which help the modern Congress assimilate the large amount of information it receives daily.

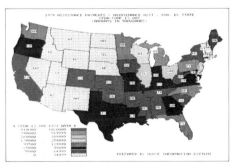

Federal assistance to States, localities, business firms and individuals is of vital interest to Senators and Representatives. Computer-generated maps are being used to present amounts of Federal moneys distributed throughout the country, program by program.

These systems and an increasing number of computer-assisted models are employed to help formulate policy alternatives, determine the long-range impact of proposed legislation and enhance the oversight capabilities of Congress.

Legislative Information and Research Systems

Increases in the magnitude and complexity of the legislative workload, and the changing legislative process, require a significant amount of record-keeping and research activities by Members, committees and staff. In response to these needs, several automated information systems have been created. Two of these systems are Legis, a computerized system which records and tracks all bills, resolutions and floor amendments, including meetings, hearings and mark-up sessions of committees, and Presidential actions on

measures which become law or are vetoed. Also in Legis are communications and messages from the Executive Branch and the President, nominations submitted by the President for the advice and consent of the Senate, and petitions and memorials from individuals and state and local governments. Another system is Sopad, an automated system which provides summaries of House Chamber proceedings within minutes of events occurring on the House Floor.

Automated Text-Editing and Electronic Printing

Through the use of automated text-editing systems Congress can now eliminate many of the tedious clerical tasks associated with editing and revising long documents. In addition, both the House and Senate now utilize the electronic printing equipment of the Government Printing Office (GPO) for bill processing, committee calendar preparation, hearings publication, the Journals and the Congressional Record. At the same time initiatives have been undertaken to improve the design of Congressional documents, to improve clarity of organization, increase readability and control costs.

Electronic Voting

Automated voting procedures were first employed in the House of Representatives in January 1973. The electronic voting system was installed in an effort to reduce the time required by the House voting process. The system shows information on votes in progress; running totals of Yea, Nay and Present responses; the time remaining

Information in Legislative Data Bases is constantly monitored for accuracy and completeness. These data bases are used for information retrieval, printed reports, and to assist in the preparation of official records of the Congress.

Millions of letters are received each year by Members of Congress. Staffs use computers to assist Senators and Representatives in their timely responses to constituents.

Members of Congress and their Committees use computer generated charts and graphs to study the performance of the American economy and to aid them in their legislative and investigative tasks.

By using a computer terminal in the office, a Congressional staff person can make an inquiry regarding the status of a piece of legislation and receive a response on the terminal's screen in a matter of seconds.

during the voting period; and the identification of the vote or quorum under consideration, on displays in the Chamber. It also assists in various clerical tasks associated with the voting process, including printing copies of the final vote results for distribution.

Administrative Support Services

Although not highly visible, a variety of automated services support administrative functions of the Congress. These activities enable the Congress to function in a more orderly and cost-effective manner. Among the administrative functions receiving computer assistance are the keeping of personnel and payroll records, vouchers, and equipment inventory files and the performance of other financial management activities.

Members and Committee Office Automation

Computer systems now provide the means to assist Member and committee offices in establishing orderly, efficient and cost-effective operations. A substantial amount of time is often required for Members to respond to constituent queries on specific legislative issues and requests for assistance. Use of automated systems for correspondence management, text preparation, document revision, financial and inventory control, and scheduling of activities has been beneficial for establishing modern management procedures in Congressional offices.

Orientation and Training

The successful employment of new technologies depends on the proper orientation and adequate training of Members and staff in their use. The House, Senate and the Congressional Research Service provide a series of cooperative comprehensive courses in retrieval of information from the variety of systems available throughout Congress. Information professionals conduct classroom sessions, including practice using computer terminal equipment, as well as distribute training manuals. Continuing education is also provided as new additions are made to Congressional data bases, and assistance is available at all times to users with computer terminal difficulties or who have general questions about system performance or resources.

Micrographics

Micrographics technology has been used on Capitol Hill for many years for archival purposes. Currently new day-to-day uses of various microforms are being actively used in Member and committee offices, as well as in such administrative units as the Secretary of the Senate, the Clerk of the House and the Architect of the Capitol. Storage of materials in microforms offers the advantages of reducing storage space, providing duplicate copies at minimal cost and eliminating certain tedious filing tasks.

Audio-Video

The use of audio and video media for transferring information has become increasingly popular within the legislative setting. Greater public interest has been expressed in the activities of the Congress and this interest has been important in the movement toward televising floor proceedings and committee hearings. The House of Representatives now makes available television coverage of its floor proceedings, and the Senate makes available audio coverage of its floor proceedings to each Senator's office. Live coverage of Senate and House hearings on topics of special interest are also broadcast on certain occasions. In the Senate, audio coverage of the floor debate on the Panama Canal Treaty in 1978 was well received by the public and served as a pilot effort in this area.

Another use of audio-video techniques is in providing briefings to Members of Congress and their staffs. The Congressional Research Service offers several of its Issue Briefs in audio cassette form and has produced a limited number of video briefings on topics of critical interest to Congress. Also of note is the potential offered by video-conferencing via satellite. This technique was successfully demonstrated in the 95th Congress when the Senate Subcommittee on Science, Technology and Space was linked to witnesses commenting on artificial weather modification situated in Springfield, Illinois. Another session provided the opportunity for a Member of Congress to talk to a group of students in his home district. As indicated by this experiment, Congress continues to explore the potential offered by new techniques and technologies for improving two-way communications between legislators and their constituents.

Automatic typewriters with memory, logic and advanced word processing capabilities are being used throughout the Congress to provide cost effective report and letter production in a quality format.

Representative Charles Rose, of North Carolina, Chairman of the Speaker's Advisory Committee on Broadcasting, has responsibility for the video broadcasting of House floor proceedings and for cable television services provided to the House of Representatives.

Congress and the President

The President addresses Congress in joint session.

The First Lady receives a warm welcome in the Executive Gallery of the House Chamber.

Courtesy Basil S. Jewell—Senate Photographic Studio.

Invitation for inaugural ceremonies sent by the Joint Congressional Committee on Inaugural Ceremonies.

The honor of your presence
is requested at the ceremonies
attending the Inauguration of the
President and Vice President
of the United States
January twentieth
Nineteen hundred eighty-one

Mark O. Hatfield, Chairman,
Howard H. Baker, Jr., Robert C. Byrd,
Claiborne Pell,
John J. Rhodes, Robert H. Michel,
Thomas P. O'Neill, Jr., Jim Wright,

Joint Congressional
Committee on Inaugural Ceremonies.

Please present the enclosed
card of admission.   11:30 A.M.

Some of the Members and Staff of the 1981 Joint Congressional Committee on Inaugural Ceremonies meet for an official portrait.

The inauguration of the 40th President of the United States, Ronald Wilson Reagan, on the West Front of the Capitol, January 20, 1981.

Mrs. Nancy Reagan and Mrs. Rosalynn Carter arrive at the Capitol with Congressional Leaders.

Then-President Jimmy Carter is updated on the Iranian hostage situation by phone in an office in the Capitol minutes prior to President Reagan's inauguration.

Senator Mark O. Hatfield of Oregon, and Senate Majority Leader Howard H. Baker, Jr. of Tennessee, escort the future President and Vice President through the Rotunda of the Capitol.

A moment of congratulations for President Reagan during the inaugural ceremonies.

The President and Vice President pause in Speaker Thomas P. O'Neill, Jr.'s office to sign an assortment of first-day covers.

A portion of the press corps covering the inaugural ceremonies.

Honored guests at the inaugural ceremonies—photograph by Senator Howard H. Baker, Jr., of Tennessee.

Chief Justice of the United States Warren E. Burger administers the Presidential oath of office to Ronald Wilson Reagan, as Mrs. Nancy Reagan holds the Bible on January 20, 1981.

Officials of the Joint Congressional Committee on Inaugural Ceremonies and Congressional Leaders escort former President Carter and Vice President Mondale through the Rotunda of the Capitol.

President Reagan delivers his inaugural speech on the West Front of the Capitol.

The late five-star General Omar Nelson Bradley attends the inaugural ceremonies.

President Reagan addresses honored guests during an inaugural day lunch in the Rotunda of the Capitol.

Vice President and Barbara Bush leaving the Capitol.

A cheerful President and First Lady depart from the Capitol for the White House.

Working Relationships

The relationship between the Congress and the President is intricate and complex. In theory, their powers and responsibilities are separated; in fact, their roles overlap. Thus, although the Constitution vests all legislative authority in the Congress, the President has important powers and responsibilities—both constitutional and customary—in the formulation and enactment of legislation. And while the Constitution gives the executive authority to the President, it also empowers Congress to check the President's actions in many ways.

Under the Constitution, the President must inform the Congress periodically on the state of the Union; he usually does so annually. The President may also transmit to Congress special messages and reports on particular subjects, and he often sends to "the Hill" actual drafts of bills. He may exercise his veto power, threaten to do so, or appeal personally and directly to Congressional leaders and individual Members of Congress to persuade them to support his programs. His authority to adjourn Congressional sessions in case of disagreement between the two

The President and Vice President meet with Congressional Leaders at the White House.

The President arrives at the Capitol with his Vice President.

The President signs his first Executive Order in the President's room of the Capitol, as the Vice President and Congressional Leaders witness the signing.

The President addresses a Joint Session of Congress.

The President makes a courtesy call on The Speaker of the House.

Houses has never been exercised, but he has occasionally used his power to call either or both Houses into "special" session, although rarely since the 1920s.

The President's state of the Union message to Congress receives wide public attention. Although the time, place and manner of transmitting it is discretionary with each President, he customarily delivers the message in person. Quite often it contains his views on significant matters requiring legislative attention and on the kind of legislation he wants Congress to enact.

With the advent of television, this annual speech has been increasingly addressed to the people of America and of the world as well as to the Congress. It is a solemn occasion of state; modern Presidents have used it to dramatize their aims and policies and to gain Congressional support for their recommendations.

Constitutionally, the President has four courses of action when Congress submits a bill or joint resolution for his signature. He may sign it into law. He may hold it for up to ten days, whereupon, if Congress is still in session, it becomes law without his signature. If Congress adjourns during the ten-day period, the measure dies if the President has failed to sign it. This "pocket veto" is absolute and cannot be overridden by the Congress. Finally, the President may veto a measure by returning it to Congress without his signature and with a statement of the reasons for his disapproval. Congress may override the President's veto by a two-thirds vote in each House, whereupon the measure becomes law without the President's signature. If Congress does not override the veto, it will often redraft the legislation and try to work with the Administration until an agreement can be reached.

Senator Paul Laxalt, of Nevada, a close friend of the President's, makes a point during a meeting with the President and Senate Republican Leaders during a meeting on the Hill.

Representative Dan Rostenkowski, of Illinois, Chairman of the Committee on Ways and Means, welcomes the President to the Capitol as House Majority Leader Jim Wright, of Texas, and Majority Whip Thomas Foley, of Washington, look on.

The President often meets informally with the leaders and other Members of Congress not only to discuss legislation, but also to exchange ideas and opinions on current events, problems and matters of importance to the Nation. Frequently, the President invites Members to the White House for briefings and sends his aides to Capitol Hill for the same purpose. The Congressional leadership is usually invited to the White House to be informed of major Presidential decisions and actions or important events before they are announced to the rest of the country and the world.

The President is welcomed to the House side of the Capitol by Silvio O. Conte, of Massachusetts, and various Congressional Leaders.

The relationship between the executive and legislative branches of our Government is sometimes marked with conflict, often characterized by compromise, and sometimes strained. Nevertheless, the two branches usually strive to work harmoniously for the best interests of the Nation.

On the Senate side of the Capitol, Senator Howard M. Metzenbaum, of Ohio, shares a few moments with the President.

Soon after delivering the state of the Union address, the President sends to Congress his annual budget message and economic report. These are normally delivered in writing rather than in person. All Presidents send numerous other special messages to the Congress at various times during a Congressional session. Ordinarily these cover some special subject and are designed and timed to enhance support for the President's legislative agenda. Occasionally the President delivers a special message in person to emphasize the subject's vital importance. He may be warning a foreign nation of possible American reaction to its behavior, or he may be interpreting or summarizing American views for the benefit of the rest of the world.

In addition to these various messages, the President and executive agencies often send draft legislation to the Congress. Members of Congress usually introduce these items at the request of the President because neither he nor any executive official may do so.

How much effect these and other Presidential actions have in persuading Congress to accept his recommendations depends upon the circumstances. Congress is under no legal obligation to follow the President's lead, and often does not. It may or may not act; if it acts, it may do so in accord with or in direct opposition to the President's stated wishes. Few major Presidential proposals survive the legislative process unchanged. Every President eventually learns that while the President proposes, the Congress disposes.

The President meets with Congressional Leaders in the President's room located in the Capitol.

The President's "Inner Circle."

1 Ronald Reagan, President

2 George Bush, Vice President

3 Alexander M. Haig, Jr., Secretary of State

4 Raymond J. Donovan, Secretary of Labor

5 Donald T. Regan, Secretary of the Treasury

6 Terrel H. Bell, Secretary of Education

7 David A. Stockman, Director of the Office of Management and Budget

8 Andrew L. Lewis, Jr., Secretary of Transportation

9 Samuel R. Pierce, Jr., Secretary of Housing and Urban Development

10 William French Smith, Attorney General

11 James G. Watt, Secretary of the Interior

12 Jeane J. Kirkpatrick, United States Representative to the United Nations

13 Edwin Meese III, Counselor to the President

14 James B. Edwards, Secretary of Energy

15 Malcolm Baldrige, Secretary of Commerce

16 William E. Brock, United States Trade Representative

17 Richard S. Schweiker, Secretary of Health and Human Services

18 John R. Block, Secretary of Agriculture

19 William J. Casey, Director of Central Intelligence

20 Caspar W. Weinberger, Secretary of Defense

Legislative Support Agencies

George M. White,
Architect of the Capitol
(left), and Daniel J.
Boorstin, Librarian of
Congress, wait to
appear before the
Senate Committee on
Rules and
Administration.

The Main Reading
Room of the Library
of Congress

Courtesy of Shepard Sherbell

Library of Congress

The Library of Congress is believed to be the largest repository of organized knowledge in the world. It was founded in 1800 to "furnish such books as may be necessary for the use of Congress."

In the gray granite structure shown on these pages, and in the neighboring John Adams and James Madison Memorial Buildings are housed more than 20 million books and pamphlets, to-

One of the Library's many treasures: the contents of Lincoln's pockets the night he died.

Daniel J. Boorstin, the Librarian of Congress.

A portion of the rare book collection.

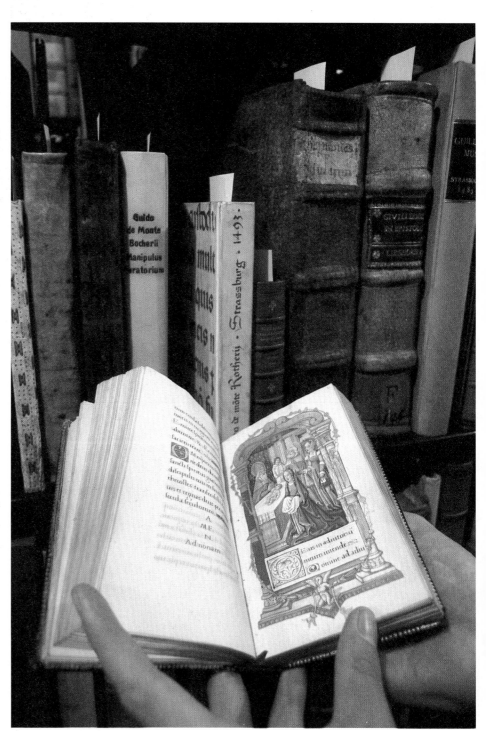

gether with more than 60 million manuscripts, maps, prints, photographs and other examples of man's graphic expression through the ages. Among the Library's greatest possessions are some of the most revered documents of American history, such as Jefferson's "rough draft" of the Declaration of Independence, one of the original copies of the Bill of Rights and the first two drafts of the Gettysburg Address in Lincoln's handwriting. From these collections can be drawn the facts that are needed to frame informed legislation.

The Library's relationship to the Congress of the United States is unique. It is an immediately accessible and indispensable tool of the Members of Congress and their committees. Its first and foremost function is to serve them. The Library furnishes facts and reports on any subject they need. Any Member or committee may borrow the book or document needed, or may have it excerpted, pinpointed or analyzed by experts on the Library staff. One department alone, the Congressional Research Service, handled more than 300,000 congressional inquiries by phone during fiscal 1980. On a busy day, it is not unusual for more than 2,000 inquiries to be received. Many other congressional requests are answered by the Law Library, research services, divisions and other departments.

The Library was housed in the Capitol until 1897. It suffered two disastrous fires early in its history. The entire collection of some 3,000 books was destroyed during the War of 1812, when British troops temporarily occupied Washington and burned the Capitol on August 24, 1814. Congress

promptly reconstituted the collections by purchasing the private library of Thomas Jefferson, some 6,000 volumes, on January 30, 1815. Jefferson had spent nearly 50 years assembling these books, which he had carefully organized with his own system of classification. From this new beginning the Library grew rapidly until December 24, 1851, when another fire destroyed about 35,000 volumes.

Since that time the Library's growth has been uninterrupted. The purchase in 1867 of the Peter Force collection of more than 60,000 books, pamphlets and other items of Americana was one of a number of notable acquisitions with which Congress enriched the collections of its Library. In 1930 Congress voted $1,500,000 for the purchase of the Vollbehr Collection of 3,000 fifteenth-century books, including the famous Gutenberg Bible,

the first book printed from movable metal type. The transfer of the library of the Smithsonian Institution to the Library of Congress in 1866, and subsequent receipts through this source, have added more than a million volumes. In 1870 Congress assigned to the Library all duties connected with copyright, insuring that it would receive a large part of the literary and artistic production of the United States. Substantial gifts from private individuals also have increased enormously the Library's resources in books and manuscripts. Finally, a network of international exchange and purchases from overseas offices have brought in material from all over the world.

This continued expansion of the collections has dictated the expansion of the Library's physical plant as well. In the spring of 1980, the Library more than doubled its available space with

During the War of 1812, the British burned the Library, which then was located in the Capitol.

James Madison Memorial Building.

The Library of Congress Thomas Jefferson Building, with the John Adams Building at the rear.

The Great Hall in the Library of Congress.

the opening of the James Madison Memorial Building, immediately south of the main building on Independence Ave., S.E. The new building is the size of a full city block. It contains numerous reading rooms, exhibit halls and facilities for book storage, in addition to a memorial hall honoring James Madison, the chief author of the Bill of Rights and fourth President of the United States.

The Library's total contents in 1980 amounted to well over 80 million items. In addition to more than 20 million printed volumes and pamphlets, there are more than 62,000 bound newspaper volumes, 291,000 motion picture reels, 1 million reels and strips of microfilm and more than 33 million manuscripts relating to American history and civilization. The remainder are maps and views, music, fine prints and photographs, posters and broadsides.

The Library administers the national program of library services for the blind and physically handicapped, providing in 1980 free loan of braille and talking books and magazines to more than half a million blind and physically handicapped persons through a nationwide network of more than 160 cooperating libraries. In addition the Library is a cultural center, where concerts and lectures are presented. It also houses the school for Capitol pages.

The Juilliard String Quartet performs frequently in the Coolidge Auditorium of the Library.

Bookbinder applying his craft in the rare book division.

Outdoor concerts are just some of the many free cultural events at the Library.

The Library of Congress is an aggregate of many libraries. Its Law Library, for instance, is among the finest in the United States. Much of its usefulness stems from the fact that new legislation grows from records of the past. This was recognized early in the Library's history when, in 1832, Congress established the law collection. Other notable collections include those of Japanese, Chinese and Russian materials, the largest outside the Orient and the Soviet Union, respectively.

Daniel J. Boorstin, a distinguished American historian, educator and prize-winning author, presides over this unique combination of facilities and services as The Librarian of Congress. Nominated by President Ford and confirmed by the Senate on September 26, 1975, Dr. Boorstin is the 12th Librarian of Congress in the institution's history.

The Library's first priority is service to the Congress. But its doors are open to all people. Anyone over high school age can use the Library's collections. Its exhibition halls are thronged with school children and other visitors. Its reading rooms attract scholars and students from all over the world. Its bibliographic, loan and catalog distribution services are used by the entire library world.

The Congressional Research Service

The Congressional Research Service, a separate department within the Library, serves as one of the research arms of the Congress. The Service was first established in 1914 for the periods during which Congress was in session. As the complexities and the burden of the problems before Congress increased, its staff and functions were enlarged accordingly, comprising today a staff of more than 800 persons, including selected experts in such fields as law, economics, political science, international relations, natural sciences and history. Senior specialists on the staff are frequently called upon to serve as consultants to Congressional committees. The Director of the Service, Gilbert Gude, is a former Maryland Congressman whose 10 years of congressional service place him in a unique position to anticipate and serve the needs of Congress.

Formerly called the Legislative Reference Service, the Congressional Research Service received its new name and greatly expanded responsibilities under legislation passed by Congress in 1970. The Service, at the beginning of each Congress, prepares and presents to each Congressional committee a list of subjects and policy areas related to its concerns and also a list of programs and activities scheduled to expire during that Congress. Upon request the Service prepares legislative histories on measures to be considered in hearings; supplies committees with experts to prepare objective, nonpartisan analyses of legislative proposals that include evaluations of whether enactment of these or alternative proposals is advisable and the probable results of each; and gathers, analyzes and makes available to Members and committees other information needed in the performance of their duties. Also prepared regularly is a comprehensive digest of bills and resolutions of a public general nature introduced in either House.

CRS "hotline" handles inquiries from Congressional offices.

Some of the various publications of the Congressional Research Service.

Gilbert Gude, Director, Congressional Research Service.

The staff of the Congressional Research Service prepare reports for Members of Congress.

Congressional Budget Office

In a major effort to reassert its constitutional authority over the Federal budget, the Congress, in 1974, enacted a comprehensive budget reform measure, the Congressional Budget and Impoundment Control Act of 1974 (Public Law 93–344). The Budget Act established a process whereby each year the Congress determines the appropriate level of Federal revenues, spending and debt, and the size of the deficit or surplus, through the passage of two concurrent resolutions on the budget.-

Each spring the Congress formulates and adopts a concurrent resolution setting budget targets for the fiscal year to begin on the coming October 1st. In September the Congress reviews the detailed spending and revenue decisions it has made since the first resolution in the form of individual bills. It then debates and adopts a second concurrent resolution, confirming or changing the totals in the spring resolution. While the first resolution sets targets, the second establishes an actual ceiling on spending and a floor for revenues. If changing circumstances require subsequent adjustments, the Congress can enact additional concurrent resolutions.

To implement this process the Budget Act created three new Congressional institutions: a Committee on the Budget in both the House and the Senate and the Congressional Budget Office (CBO). CBO is a nonpartisan organization mandated to provide the Congress with budget-related information and with analyses of alternative fiscal and programmatic policies. The office does not make recommendations on matters of policy. Its principal tasks are to present the Congress with options for consideration and to study the possible budgetary ramifications of those options.

The organization is headed by a Director who is appointed to a four-year term by the Speaker of the House and the President Pro Tempore of the Senate, after considering the recommendations of the Budget Committees. Dr. Alice Rivlin was named the first Director of CBO in February 1975 and reappointed in 1979. For fiscal year 1980, CBO was authorized a budget of $12,386,000 and a staff of 218 persons.

The Budget Act requires CBO to provide cost estimates on proposed legislation.

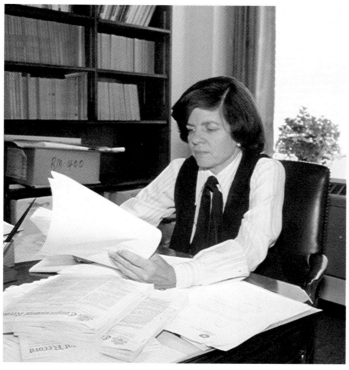

Alice M. Rivlin, Director
Congressional Budget
Office.

CBO prepares, to the extent practicable, a five-year estimate of what it would cost the Federal Government to carry out any public bill or resolution reported by a Congressional committee. These estimates include projections of new or increased tax expenditures and new budget authority when applicable. CBO compares its cost estimates with any estimates available from Congressional committees or Federal agencies.

As soon as practicable after the beginning of each fiscal year, CBO prepares a report that projects Federal revenues and spending for the next five years, if current laws and policies were to continue unchanged. The purpose of these projections is to provide a neutral baseline against which the Congress can consider potential changes as it examines the budget for the upcoming fiscal years.

CBO keeps track, or score, of Congressional action on individual appropriation and revenue bills against the targets or ceilings in the concurrent resolutions. The office issues periodic reports showing the status of Congressional action.

Since the Federal budget both affects and is affected by the national economy, the Congress must consider the budget in the context of the current and projected state of the economy. To provide a framework for such considerations, CBO prepares periodic analyses and forecasts of economic trends. The office also prepares analyses of alternative fiscal policies.

CBO undertakes analyses of programmatic or policy issues that affect the Federal budget. These reports include an examination of alternative approaches to current policy. All reports are nonpartisan in nature. Major studies have been completed in such diverse areas as agriculture, energy, housing, hospital and medical costs, defense, state and local government, employment programs, transportation, education, budget procedures, international economic policy, taxation, child nutrition and ways to cut government spending.

CBO prepares estimates of the inflationary effect of major legislative proposals. More generally, the office is charged with identifying and analyzing the causes of inflation.

By April 1 of each year, CBO furnishes a report to the House and Senate Committees on the Budget that combines many aspects of the functions outlined above.

CBO prepares its studies and cost estimates at the request of the chairman or ranking minority member of a full committee of jurisdiction or the chairman of a subcommittee of jurisdiction. The Budget Act establishes the following priority for these services: first, the Senate and House Budget Committees; second, the Senate and House Appropriations Committees, the Senate Finance Committee, and the House Ways and Means Committee; finally, all other Congressional committees.

CBO's published reports are distributed to all Members of Congress. A list of the publications is available from CBO's Office of Intergovernmental Relations, and most of the publications can be obtained either directly from CBO or, for a small fee, from the Superintendent of Documents, U.S. Government Printing Office, Washington, DC 20402.

CBO staff review a committee transcript regarding Federal appropriations.

Some of the various publications of the Congressional Budget Office.

CBO staff review computer reports on budget details.

CBO is located in a Congressional Office Building along with other House Committee offices.

General Accounting Office

GAO publications are important informative and analytical documents for Congressional oversight.

GAO's Headquarters Building is the base from which its staff conducts reviews of Federal programs worldwide. Its location is convenient both to Capitol Hill and Cabinet department offices.

Finding ways to run the Federal Government—a $600 billion enterprise—more efficiently, effectively and economically is the task of the U.S. General Accounting Office.

The General Accounting Office came into existence as an independent, nonpolitical arm of the Congress in 1921 when the Budget and Accounting Act was enacted.

GAO's basic purposes are:

—To assist the Congress, its committees and its Members as much as possible in carrying out their legislative and oversight responsibilities, consistent with the agency's role as an independent, nonpolitical agency.

—To audit and evaluate the programs, activities and financial operations of Federal departments and agencies and make recommendations toward more efficient and effective operations.

—To carry out financial control and other functions with respect to Federal Government programs and operations including accounting, legal and claims settlement work.

GAO's primary internal objective is to perform all of its functions as effectively, efficiently, economically and promptly as possible.

Government has become much more complex since the Congress established GAO 60 years ago. The needs of the Congress for help have grown and will continue to grow.

This agency's greatest contribution is to provide answers to questions such as:

—Where are there opportunities to eliminate fraud, waste and abuse in government?

—Are Federal programs, whether administered directly by the Federal Government or through other organizations, such as the United Nations, or through State and local governments, achieving their objectives?

—Are there other ways of accomplishing the objectives of these programs at lower costs?

—Are funds being spent legally and is the accounting for them adequate?

Using such information, Members of Congress are in a better position to make decisions concerning Government programs—whether the issue is continuing an innovative education program, acquiring a major weapons system for the Defense Department or providing development assistance for a foreign country.

Concerns are being voiced in the Congress and elsewhere about the apparent decrease of confidence in the Govenment, particularly in the Government's ability to make programs effective and to serve well those individuals and groups for whom public funds are spent. Greater attention is also being focused on the accountability of Government officials to taxpayers. Thus it is more important than ever that the public be aware of the work of GAO as an organization with principal concern for fiscal integrity and the economical and effective management of Government programs.

Another concern frequently expressed in the Congress is that the executive branch has increased its power in relationship to the legislative branch for the simple reason that the executive branch has most of the experts and information on such complex subjects as major weapons systems, energy, space exploration, health care, and pollution control.

Many of these experts and much of the information from the executive branch are made available to the Congress through hearings and reports, or by less formal means. However, inevitable questions remain.

—Were the proper alternatives to proposed programs fully considered and set forth objectively to the Congress?
—Does the executive branch keep the Congress adequately advised on progress and on problems which develop as programs are carried out?
—Does the information provided facilitate, rather than frustrate, legislative oversight?

Accordingly, one of GAO's objectives is to strengthen the processes through which the Congress can obtain reliable information.

Public Responsibility

In a broad context, the agency is responsible to the public. GAO reports to the Congress, if not classified for national security reasons, are public reports. Although GAO has no official ombudsman responsibility, it tries at all times to be sensitive to responsible criticisms of Federal programs and to take these criticisms into account in planning its work.

GAO does not seek publicity for its reports. But it is important that the public have full access to its findings and conclusions.

The agency recognizes that certain information must be classified in the interest of national security. The legal authority to classify information rests with the operating agencies. GAO has as one of its objectives, however, the questioning of security classifications which seem unnecessary for the purposes of security legislation and regulations.

The organization's role will continue to change as the needs of the Congress respond to the increasing size and complexity of our Nation and its Government.

GAO performs much of its work with the objective of improving Government operations. As a result of its recommendations, Federal agencies take many actions to make their programs and services more economical and effective.

It is not possible to determine the full effect of GAO activities in terms of financial savings, improvements in Government operations, and increased effectiveness of Government programs and activities. However, GAO attempts to record actions attributable to its work which result in dollar savings or other benefits to the Federal Govern-

ment, contractors, grantees and the general public. These actions may be taken directly by the agency, as in the case of claims collections. Usually, however, they are taken by the Congress, Federal agencies and others, in response to suggestions and recommendations.

For fiscal year 1980, GAO identified estimated savings of $3.7 billion attributable to its work. At the same time, it should be remembered that many accomplishments cannot always be stated in precise dollar terms. Savings resulting from management improvements often cannot be measured accurately, nor can improvements which make programs work better but not cheaper. Such improvements are often more important than simple financial savings.

Early in its history, most GAO employees were accountants or auditors who spent long hours pouring over vouchers and other financial records of Government agencies. However, in the 1950s, the organization extended the scope of its reviews to include:
—checking for compliance with applicable laws and regulations,
—examining the efficiency and economy of operations, and
—reviewing the results of operations of evaluating whether desired results, including legislatively prescribed objectives, have been effectively achieved.

In the past years, GAO's professional staff—numbering 4,200—has been expanded to include engineers, mathematicians, statisticians, computer specialists, economists, business and public administrators, and even a medical doctor.

During fiscal year 1980, the agency issued 935 audit reports and special studies, addressed to the Congress, its committees or Members, or to heads of departments and agencies. Copies of these reports are available to the public through GAO's Distribution Section, Room 1518, 441 G Street, NW, Washington, D.C. 20548.

GAO provides information to the Congress by testifying before Congressional committees; holding informal briefings on agency problems for committees, Members and staffs; assigning staff members to work on Congressional committees; and providing legal opinions and comments on pending legislation.

In addition, the Office undertakes reviews of major Government programs on its own initiative. Although GAO is authorized to investigate all matters relating to the receipt, dis-

bursement, and application of public funds (with some exceptions), the policy is to review programs, activities, or functions of direct interest to the Congress and the public.

Other GAO Responsibilities

GAO prescribes principles and standards for accounting in executive branch agencies, and cooperates with the agencies in developing and improving their accounting and financial management systems.

The office settles legal questions concerning the legality of planned expenditures of Federal funds.

Questions over the award of Government contracts may prompt requests for a Comptroller General ruling on the bid protest. GAO decisions on questions about the award of Government contracts are binding on the executive branch, but may be overturned by the Congress or the courts.

The agency also settles claims for or against the Government. Claims which involve no doubtful questions of law are paid or collected by the agency involved, subject to GAO audit.

Some Further Facts About GAO

The Comptroller General of the United States is the head of GAO. The Comptroller General is appointed by the President, with the advice and consent of the Senate, to a 15-year term— the longest set term in the Federal Government. He cannot be removed except for cause. These provisions guarantee his independence from political influence.

The Comptroller General heads an operation that includes the headquarters office and 83 audit sites, 15 regional offices in the continental United States and branch offices in Bangkok, Frankfurt, Honolulu, and Panama City.

Government Printing Office

Virtually in the shadow of the Capitol stands the United States Government Printing Office. This four-building complex at North Capitol and H Streets houses an impressive array of production equipment as well as warehousing for paper, laboratories for testing graphic arts materials, facilities for rail and motor shipping, and administrative offices. In all, 34 acres of floor space are used in this location. Another 20-plus acres of publications distribution and paper warehousing are rented in various locations. The Government Printing Office also operates five Regional Field Printing plants and 14 Regional Printing Procurement Offices throughout the United States.

The Government Printing Office began operation in 1861 to produce all printing, binding, and blank book work for Congress, the Executive Office, the Judiciary, other than the Supreme Court of the United States, and every executive department, independent office and establishment of the Federal Government. Buildings, equipment and machinery were acquired from Cornelius Wendell, a private printer, for $135,000. The original plant stood on the site now occupied by the newest of GPO's buildings and was staffed by a work force of 350. Today GPO employs more than 6,600 employees.

Senator Charles McC. Mathias, Jr., right, of Maryland and Representative Augustus F. Hawkins of California serve as the Chairman and the Vice Chairman of the Joint Committee on Printing which is GPO's governing body.

The Government Printing Office, which produces the *Congressional Record* among its many printing requirements, is almost within the shadow of the Capitol.

Liaison between the Government Printing Office and the Congress is accomplished by the Congressional Information Division at the GPO.

Chairman of the Senate Committee on Rules and Administration, Senator Charles McC. Mathias, Jr., right, of Maryland welcomes Public Printer Danford L. Sawyer, Jr., at his hearing.

In fiscal year 1980 the products and services provided by GPO amounted to over $775 million. Of this amount, nearly $475 million of printing was procured from commercial firms which compete on the basis of price and service for Government work.

To meet the printing and binding needs of its more than 120 customers, all of which are agencies of the Federal Government, the Office operates 70 presses of various kinds. It utilizes conventional "hot-metal" typesetting equipment as well as the most modern computer text processing and electronic photocomposition systems. These include 14 Text Editing Systems with over 175 video display terminals. High speed CRT phototypesetting systems include three VideoComp 500's, a Linotron 1010 (both used for full page and galley output), and one Comp 80/2 which is utilized to produce full page output onto microform. Stand alone systems include one Compugraphic Editwriter 7500. A total of 230 binding machines such as cutters, stitchers, gatherers and sewing machines are used to manufacture finished documents and hard-bound books.

The GPO operates around the clock, the needs of Congress comprising the most important of its nighttime production. Foremost among those needs is printing the indispensable Proceedings and Debates of the Congress, better known as the *Congressional Record*. This publication, printed each day when either of the Houses is in session, currently averages more than 200 pages daily. It consists of four main parts: a chronicle of floor action in the Senate, the same for the House, an Extension of Remarks and a Daily Digest. The Extension portion carries official and unofficial material pertinent to, but not properly a part of, chamber proceedings. The Daily Digest lists the highlights of current legislative business, committee meetings and the legislative program ahead. About 31,000 copies of the *Record* are produced daily from newly set type.

Copy begins flowing to the GPO around 6:00 p.m. each day and concurrently the GPO production staff begins building up to accommodate the influx. By midnight, all copy is supposed to be in the Office but at times this deadline is exceeded by late-arriving material. It is not uncommon for every one of GPO's composing machines to be manned in order to get all copy set into type in sufficient time to allow for

plating, press-running time and finishing operations. All operations are keyed to meeting fixed early morning delivery schedules which insure that Members of Congress and their staffs receive copies of the *Record* promptly.

During the day, type for a similar publication—the *Federal Register*—is set by computerized photocomposition. The *Register* contains presidential proclamations and executive orders, as well as Federal agency regulations and notices. Averaging 320 pages and 52,000 copies, the *Register* also has a daily delivery requirement.

The Government Printing Office not only carries out its printing and publications functions, it also operates a sizable distribution and sales program. The Documents area, established in 1895 as an organic part of the GPO, performs this function. In Fiscal 1980 this department distributed nearly 136 million publications, including nearly 20 million to Depository Libraries, and sold nearly 45 million documents to the public, chiefly through its mail order service. Twenty-seven bookstores, 20 of which are located outside metropolitan Washington area, sold nearly $8 million worth of publications. The Office of the Superintendent of Documents Department's income was nearly $48 million from mail order and bookstore sales.

The GPO, properly called the largest general printing plant in the world under one roof, averages in excess of 1,800 new orders daily. Federal printing is directly responsive to the needs of the Government and as America grows and prospers its progress will continue to be mirrored in its printing.

More and more government printing is being produced electronically, and at the Government Printing Office there is perhaps the most comprehensive electronic photo-composition equipment under one roof anywhere.

Typography and Design Division conferring on design for this issue of The Capitol.

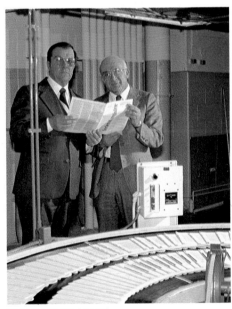

Archivist of the United States Robert Warner and Acting Public Printer Samuel L. Saylor (ret.) reviewing production of the *Federal Register*.

In addition to some 27,000 annual requests for publications as well as for information, the Government Printing Office handles countless telephone calls in its Documents Information Center.

Office of Technology Assessment

Chairman: Senator Ted Stevens of Alaska.

The Office of Technology Assessment (OTA) is a nonpartisan analytical support agency created in 1972 to serve the Congress (Public Law 92–484). OTA's job is to analyze complex issues involving science and technology for both the Senate and House Committees. It clarifies the range of policy options on a given issue and the potential physical, biological, economic, social and political impacts of adopting each of these options. OTA does not advocate particular policies or actions.

A 12-member bipartisan Congressional Board—six Senators and six Representatives—governs OTA. Senator Ted Stevens (R-Alaska) is Chairman and Representative Morris K. Udall (D-Ariz.) is Vice Chairman for the 97th Congress. These posts alternate between the Senate and House with each Congress.

The Board appoints the OTA Director, who is chief executive officer and a nonvoting Board member. Dr. John H. Gibbons, nationally known scientist, has served as Director since June, 1979. Prior to his appointment, Dr. Gibbons directed the Energy, Environment and Resources Center at the University of Tennessee. He was the first director of the energy conservation programs of the Federal Energy Administration (FEA). Dr. Gibbons also spent 18 years at Oak Ridge National Laboratory, where he conducted research and led several national studies of energy and environmental issues. He holds a doctorate in physics from Duke University.

The Congressional Board is assisted by an Advisory Council comprised of 10 citizens from the private sector and, ex officio, the Comptroller General of the United States and the Director of the Congressional Research Service of the Library of Congress.

The Chairman of the Advisory Council is Dr. Charles N. Kimball, president emeritus and former Chairman of the Board of the Midwest Research Institute. The Council's Vice Chairman is Jerome B. Wiesner, former President of the Massachusetts Institute of Technology and former Presidential Science Advisor.

OTA has three assessment divisions, each headed by an Assistant Director: Energy, Materials and International Security, under Lionel S. Johns; Health and Life Sciences, under Joyce Lashof;

Vice Chairman: Representative Morris K. Udall of Arizona.

Dr. John H. Gibbons, Director of OTA

The OTA Congressional Board.

and Science, Information and Natural Resources, under John P. Andelin, Jr. Within these divisions are nine general program areas: energy, international security and commerce, materials, food and renewable resources, health, human resources, communication and information technologies, oceans and environment, and space technology.

OTA has a relatively small in-house staff of 80 to 90 professionals whose skills span the range of physical, life and social sciences; engineering; law and medicine. Throughout each project OTA uses advisory panels of experts and representatives of major parties-at-interest as a way of ensuring that reports are nonduplicative, objective, fair and authoritative. OTA draws extensively on the broad spectrum of resources throughout the private sector.

Last year the agency completed studies on a number of issues, including: impact of advanced group rapid transit technology; alternative energy futures, part 1—the future of liquefied natural gas imports; impact of advanced air transport technology, part 1—advanced high-speed aircraft; recent developments in ocean thermal energy; taggants in explosives; forecasts of physician supply and requirements; ocean margin drilling; oil shale technologies; a critique on conservation and solar energy programs of the Department of Energy; technology and steel industry competitiveness; energy from biological processes; the implications of cost-effectiveness analysis of medical technology; and world petroleum availability, 1980–2000.

OTA reports are available to the public through the U.S. Government Printing Office and the National Technical Information Service. Call OTA Publications Office for a list of publications and ordering information—(202) 224–8996.

Selected publications of OTA.

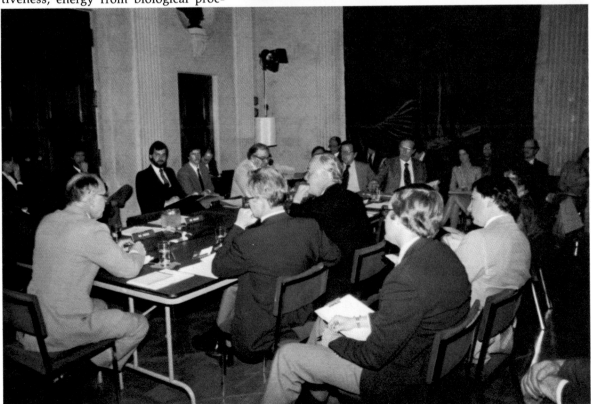

Public participation meeting at OTA.

In Highest Tribute

There is no more appropriate place than the Rotunda of the Capitol to give honor to great servants of the people.

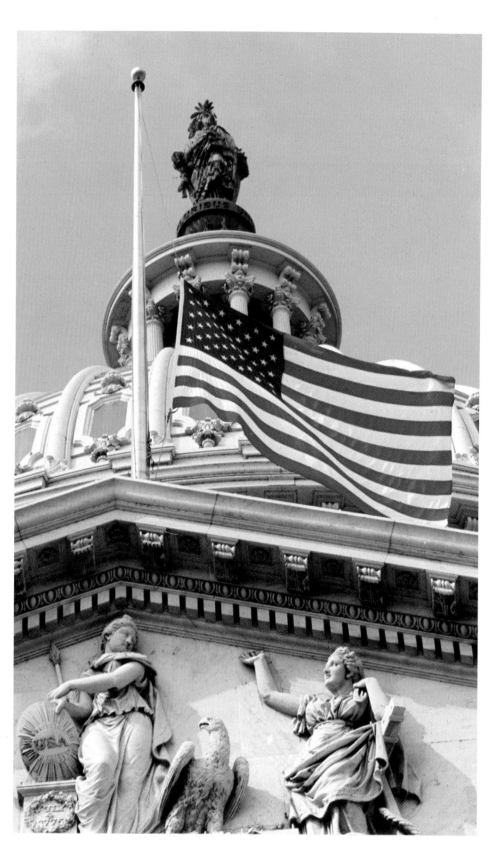

Flag at half mast over Capitol in highest tribute.

Four times in our history assassination has claimed the occupant of the White House. A forced but orderly transition took place after the tragic deaths of Abraham Lincoln, James A. Garfield, William McKinley and John F. Kennedy. All lay in state in the Rotunda of the Capitol while a grieving Nation paid them tribute.

There are no known pictures of Lincoln's services in the Capitol, but there are photographs showing all of the East Front columns circled with black bands and tied with large black bows to indicate that the Capitol was in mourning. After the death of Garfield on September 19th, 1881, *The Evening Critic,* a Washington paper, proclaimed in black-edged columns: "God Reigns. Clouds and Darkness May Surround Us, But the Government at Washington Will Live."

No black drapery appeared on public buildings in 1901 at the time of the assassination of William McKinley. A law had been passed prohibiting such decorations because of the increasing frequency of their use to mark the deaths of minor government officials. The decorations in the Rotunda planned for McKinley's lying-in-state would have been strikingly different had they been carried out. According to one newspaper report, a canopy circled with a cluster of electric lights had been built over the catafalque "so that the features of the dead president could be clearly seen" during the evening. However, a change in plans caused the viewing to close at dusk, so the electrified canopy was removed and the catafalque appeared "as it had been used by Lincoln and Garfield."

There is no law, written rule or regulation governing who may lie in state in the Rotunda. Use of the Rotunda is controlled, generally, by concurrent action of the Senate and House. However, the Rotunda has been used without full concurrence of both Houses, especially during adjournment or recess. The wishes of the family of a great individual are also respected by Congress.

There is no more appropriate place than the Rotunda of the Capitol to give honor to great servants of the people. In addition to the four Presidents who were killed while in office, there have been other Presidents and ex-Presidents accorded this same honor: Warren G. Harding in 1921, William Howard Taft in 1930, Herbert Hoover in 1964, Dwight D. Eisenhower in 1969, and Lyndon Baines Johnson in 1973. All have lain on the historic catafalque that was made for Abraham Lincoln. A total of twenty-four persons, including Senators, Representatives, and the Unknown Soldiers from World War I, World War II and Korea, have lain on the catafalque in the Rotunda to be given this high tribute by a grateful people.

President Jimmy Carter consoles Mrs. Hubert H. Humphrey during funeral ceremonies in the Capitol Rotunda.

Military honors. The horse drawn caisson and the riderless horse with the boots turned backward are two traditional symbols in a military funeral. The flag draped casket of former President Hoover is being removed from the caisson to be carried up the Senate steps and then to the Rotunda.

Those Who Have Lain in State in the Rotunda

Floral tribute. Indicative of the era when President Garfield was assassinated in 1881 were the elaborate decorations seen here around the casket in the Rotunda. This particular floral arrangement is referred to as the "Gate of Heaven" and parts of it have been preserved by the Smithsonian Institution.

Lying in state— John Fitzgerald Kennedy.

Henry Clay: Lay in state in the Rotunda, July 1, 1852, following funeral service in Old Senate Chamber. Member of U.S. Senate from Kentucky four terms (not consecutive) from 1806 to 1852; Secretary of State 1825–1829; Member of House of Representatives seven terms (not consecutive) from 1811 to 1825. During his terms in the House, he also served as Speaker, 1811–1814, 1815–1820, 1823–1825. Died June 29, 1852, in Washington, D.C.

Abraham Lincoln: Lay in state in the Rotunda, April 19–21, 1865. President of United States March 4, 1861, until his death. Member of House of Representatives from Illinois, March 4, 1847 to March 3, 1849. Shot by assassin April 14, 1865, in Washington, D.C. and died there April 15, 1865.

Thaddeus Stevens: Lay in state in the Rotunda, August 13–14, 1868, prior to funeral service in Rotunda. Member of House of Representatives from Pennsylvania, March 4, 1849 to March 3, 1853, and again from March 4, 1859, until his death. Died, August 11, 1868, in Washington, D.C.

Charles Sumner: Lay in state in the Rotunda, March 13, 1874, prior to funeral service in Senate Chamber. Member of U.S. Senate from Massachusetts, April 24, 1851, until his death. Died March 11, 1874, in Washington, D.C.

Henry Wilson: Lay in state in the Rotunda, November 25–26, 1875, prior to funeral service in Senate Chamber. Vice President of United States, March 4, 1873, until his death. Member of U.S. Senate from Massachusetts, January 31, 1855 to March 3, 1873, when he resigned to become Vice President. Died November 22, 1875, in Vice President's room in Capitol, Washington, D.C.

James Abram Garfield: Lay in state in the Rotunda, September 21–23, 1881, prior to funeral service in the Rotunda. President of United States, March 4, 1881 until his death. Member of House of Representatives from Ohio, March 4, 1863 to November 8, 1880, when he resigned, having been elected President. Shot by assassin, July 2, 1881, in Washington, D.C., and died September 19, 1881, in Elberon, New Jersey.

John Alexander Logan: Lay in state in the Rotunda, December 30–31, 1886, prior to funeral service in Senate Chamber. Member of House of Representatives from Illinois, March 4, 1859 to April 2, 1862, when he resigned to enter the Union Army, and again from March 4, 1867, until resignation on March 3, 1871, when elected Senator. Member of U.S. Senate, March 4, 1871 to March 3, 1877. Died December 26, 1886, in Washington, D.C.

William McKinley, Jr.: Lay in state in the Rotunda, September 17, 1901, following funeral in Rotunda. President of United States, March 4, 1897, until his death. Member of House of Representatives from Ohio, March 4, 1877 to May 27, 1884, and again from March 4, 1885 to March 3, 1891. Shot by assassin September 6, 1901, in Buffalo, New York, and died there September 14, 1901.

Major Pierre Charles L'Enfant (reinterment): Lay in state in the Rotunda, April 28, 1909, prior to memorial service in the Rotunda. Planner of city of Washington, D.C. Died June 4, 1825, and was buried on Digges farm, Prince Georges County, Maryland. Remains were brought to Capitol April 28, 1909. Remains were reinterred in Arlington National Cemetery.

Admiral George Dewey: Lay in state in the Rotunda, January 20, 1917, during funeral service in the Rotunda. Admiral of the Navy and hero of Manila Bay in Spanish-American War. Died January 16, 1917, in Washington, D.C.

Unknown Soldier of World War I: Lay in state in the Rotunda, November 9–11, 1921. Chosen to honor and perpetuate the memory of the heroes who gave their lives in World War I. The body is that of an unknown American who served as a member of the American Expeditionary Forces in Europe and lost his life during World War I.

Warren Gamaliel Harding: Lay in state in the Rotunda, August 8, 1923, following funeral service in the Rotunda. President of United States, March 4, 1921, until his death. Member of U.S. Senate from Ohio, March 4, 1915 to January 13, 1921, when he resigned, having been elected President. Died August 2, 1923, in San Francisco, California.

Mrs. John F. Kennedy entering the Capitol Rotunda with the late Senator Robert Kennedy and Senator Edward Kennedy of Massachusetts for memorial services.

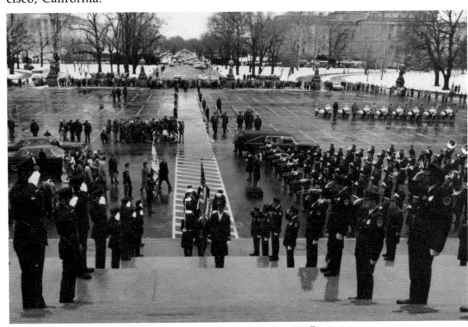

Arrival on the East Front of the Capitol with the Library of Congress and Supreme Court in the background.

189

William Howard Taft: Lay in state in the Rotunda, March 11, 1930. President of United States, March 4, 1909 to March 4, 1913. Chief Justice of U.S. Supreme Court, June 30, 1921 (commission), July 11, 1921 (oath of office) to February 3, 1930. Only man who served both as President and Chief Justice. Died March 8, 1930, in Washington, D.C.

General John Joseph Pershing: Lay in state in the Rotunda, July 18–19, 1948. General of the Armies of United States. Was graduated from U.S. Military Academy at West Point in 1886 and devoted his entire life to military service. Chief of Staff of the Army 1921–1924; Commander of American Expeditionary Forces, World War I; distinguished service during Philippine insurrection; and took part in Spanish-American War. Died July 15, 1948, in Washington, D.C.

Robert Alphonso Taft: Lay in state in the Rotunda, August 2–3, 1953, prior to memorial service in the Rotunda. Member of U.S. Senate from Ohio, January 3, 1939, until his death. Died July 31, 1953, in New York City.

Unknown Soldiers of World War II and the Korean War: Lay in state in the Rotunda, May 28–30, 1958. Chosen to honor and perpetuate the memory of the heroes who gave their lives while serving overseas in the armed forces of the U.S. during World War II and the Korean War, and whose identities are unknown.

John Fitzgerald Kennedy: Lay in state in the Rotunda, November 24–25, 1963, following memorial service in the Rotunda. President of United States, January 20, 1961, until his death. Member of House of Representatives from Massachusetts, January 3, 1947 to January 3, 1953. Member of U.S. Senate, January 3, 1953 to December 22, 1960, when he resigned having been elected President. Shot by assassin November 22, 1963, in Dallas, Texas, and died there.

General Douglas MacArthur: Lay in state in the Rotunda, April 8–9, 1964. Appointed General of the Army, December 18, 1944; Superintendent of U.S. Military Academy at West Point, 1919–1922; appointed Chief of Staff of the Army November 21, 1930. From July 26, 1941 through April 11, 1951, he served in Pacific and Far East in various allied commands. Died April 5, 1964, in Washington, D.C.

Herbert Clark Hoover: Lay in state in the Rotunda, October 23–25, 1964. President of United States, March 4, 1929 to March 3, 1933. Secretary of Commerce in cabinets of both Presidents Harding and Coolidge. Food Administrator under President Wilson, Chairman of Commission of Organization of Executive Branch of Government in 1947–1949 and 1953–1955. Died October 20, 1964, in New York City.

Dwight David Eisenhower: Lay in state in the Rotunda, March 30–31, 1969. President of United States, January 20, 1953 to January 20, 1961. Was graduated from U.S. Military Academy at West Point in 1915; promoted to General of the Army, 1944; named president of Columbia University, 1948. Died March 28, 1969, in Washington, D.C.

Everett McKinley Dirksen: Lay in state in the Rotunda, September 9–10, 1969, following memorial service in the Rotunda. Member of U.S. Senate from Illinois January 3, 1951, until his death. Member of House of Representatives, March 4, 1933 to January 3, 1949. Died September 7, 1969, in Washington, D.C.

J. Edgar Hoover: Lay in state in the Rotunda, May 3–4, 1972, following memorial service in the Rotunda. First Director of the Federal Bureau of Investigation, 1924 until his death. Died May 2, 1972, in Washington, D.C.

Lying in state—
Dwight David
Eisenhower.

Lyndon Baines Johnson: Lay in state in the Rotunda, January 24–25, 1973, following memorial service in the Rotunda. President of United States, November 22, 1963 to January 20, 1969. Member of House of Representatives from Texas, April 10, 1937 to January 3, 1949. Member of U.S. Senate, January 3, 1949 to January 3, 1961, when he resigned, having been elected Vice President. Vice President, January 20, 1961 to November 22, 1963. Died January 22, 1973, at his ranch near Johnson City, Texas.

Hubert Horatio Humphrey: Lay in state in the Rotunda, January 14–15, 1978. Member of U.S. Senate from Minnesota, November 3, 1970, until his death. Member U.S. Senate, January 3, 1949 to December 29, 1964, when he resigned to become Vice President, January 20, 1965 to January 20, 1969. Died at his home in Waverly, Minnesota.

The services for the Honorable Hubert H. Humphrey were typical of the stirring simplicity of funerals in the Rotunda. The precision of the military honor guard, the lines of people, and the now ever present TV camera can be considered a pattern for funerals in the Capitol Rotunda.

Lying in state— Lyndon Baines Johnson.

Natalie's address:
610 East Capitol St. **Credits** *#G2*
Washington, D.C. 20003
(w) 202 - 224-0307
(h) 202 - 544-4306

Editor, Eighth Edition

Gerald R. Gereau,
Professional Staff Member,
Senate Committee on Rules
and Administration.

As Editor of this publication, I am extremely grateful to the many persons and organizations who assisted through research and photography. Though I would like to identify each photograph individually, there are so many sources involved that this is next to impossible. The following list shows many of the sources from which the pictures were gathered:

John C. Ahlers
Architect of the Capitol
Armed Services Bands
Asman Custom Photo Service
Senator Howard H. Baker, Jr.
Broadcasting Magazine
Robert C. Cantrell Collection
Congressional Research Service
Corcoran Gallery of Art
Jerry David
John O. Hamilton
Louis Hollis
House Photographic Studios
Kiplinger Collection
Kodak
Library of Congress
Fred J. Maroon
Cynthia Watkins Meadow
National Archives
National Geographic Society
National Symphony
National Woman's Party
Raymond N. Nelson
Newsweek
Toby Pyle
Roloc
Dolly Seelmeyer
Senate Curator of Art and Antiquities
Senate Historian
Senate Photographic Studio
Smithsonian Institution
United States Capitol Historical Society
Office of the Vice President
White House Photography Office

In addition, those listed below comprise a select group of individuals who gave their expertise in many ways and without whose efforts this publication would not have been possible. To them I extend my gratitude for their efforts:

John C. Ahlers
Mildred L. Amer
Mark Blair
Sandra Burke
Harry L. Burnett, Jr.
Linda Burrow
Horace J. Chase
John Childers
William McWhorter Cochrane
Ann Cook
Joseph diGenova
Elizabeth M. Daoust
Hugh G. Duffy
Mark Eller
Mary Gereau
Cheryl Goode
G.P.O.—Congressional Information Division
G.P.O.—Electronic Photocomposition Division
G.P.O.—Printing and Procurement Department
G.P.O.—Typography and Design Division
Anthony Louis Harvey
Keith Jewell
Cynthia Johnston
Sal Lacapria
John Morris
Fred Mosedale
Linda Nave
Alan E. Porter
Bill Rawley
Billie Shaddix
Shepard Sherbell
Carole Stevenson
John Swearingen
Florian Thayn

FOR SALE BY THE SUPERINTENDENT OF DOCUMENTS,
U.S. GOVERNMENT PRINTING OFFICE, WASHINGTON, D.C. 20402

☆ U.S. GOVERNMENT PRINTING OFFICE : 1981 O—68-190